THE CATALOGUE OF

JEFFREY FEINMAN

Illustrations by Ivor Parry

SIMON AND SCHUSTER
New York

Designed by Stan Drate
Manufactured in the United States of America
Printed and bound by The Murray Printing Company
1   2   3   4   5   6   7   8   9   10

Library of Congress Cataloging in Publication Data

Feinman, Jeffrey.
The catalogue of magic.

1. Conjuring—Apparatus and supplies—Catalogs.
I. Title.
GV1561.F44   793.8'028   78-13128

ISBN 0-671-23107-3
ISBN 0-671-24650-X Pbk.

ACKNOWLEDGMENT

Special thanks to Sanford Kartzman, whose research, effort and friendship made this idea a reality

CONTENTS

NOTE TO
THE READER

Even if you're a person who skips introductions, we hope you'll read this: *Please don't order from this book. The Catalogue of Magic* took over eighteen months to complete. Even in normal times some prices would be inaccurate, but during the inflationary seventies, most prices will increase. They are provided for guidelines only. Also, many of these firms are small businesses. Some will survive and grow—others will (unfortunately) be out of business on or before publication date. In short, *before ordering anything, write for complete details.*

Where a catalogue is mentioned, it's a good idea to write for the catalogue first. If a charge is indicated, be sure to include payment. It becomes prohibitively expensive for many small manufacturers to send catalogues without charge.

One last note on ordering: many of the firms listed are exclusively mail-order ventures. Some actually operate part time. Therefore, if you live near an address listed, don't drop by unless you call first.

About Listings

This book is intended as a guide. We have used sources we believe to be reliable. However, listing in the book is not intended to be an endorsement. The rules of fair play and the rather strong hand of the postal authorities should assure you of honest dealing. However, we cannot guarantee any source, the address, or the information.

About Suppliers

Most tend to be smaller firms. Most suppliers were magicians first who started producing kits for friends and neighbors, then graduated to mail order. We mention this only so you'll understand if delays occur. Some firms may be inundated with requests from this catalogue and unable to answer. Sometimes you'll be required to wait longer than you'd like, to receive the item you've ordered. Please be patient.

About Future Editions

The future only points to more and more kits. Almost every supplier we spoke with had planned additions to the line. We count on our readers' help in the updating process. Readers are asked to submit ideas and comments to Jeffrey Feinman, Ventura Associates, 101 Park Avenue, New York, N.Y. 10017.

One reminder: Revealing magic secrets is considered to be unethical. More important, it's simply not very much fun in the long run. Part of magic is the mystery. Also, since the real item that is being sold each time is not only the equipment but the secret of how it works, magic shops routinely have a policy of not offering refunds. Refunds are generally offered only if the merchandise is defective or if there has been some error.

If you have any questions about the item you are planning to buy, it is best to write first. As many of the companies listed are small, it's always best to enclose a self-addressed stamped envelope.

MAGIC—AN ANCIENT ART IN A MODERN WORLD

Magic. The very sound of the word conjures up for us an atmosphere of excitement, a feeling of anticipation. Throughout history, magic has been more than an entertainment. It's been part of the fabric of life—woven into science, the governing classes, religious beliefs. Every age has had its sorcerers, wizards, and magicians almost until the twentieth century. Magicians are still with us, but now we call them engineers and scientists—men and women who perform miracles by building bridges and buildings, converting raw materials into energy, sending men to the moon. Arthur C. Clarke once noted, "Any technology that is sufficiently advanced is indistinguishable from magic."

The reality of our technological and scientific magic is overwhelming. The breakthroughs come almost too quickly for us to adjust to them and assimilate their meaning. Perhaps that's why there has been a renaissance of prestidigitation, illusion, mentalism—all the skills of magic, all the fun.

Whatever the reasons, there are new magic enthusiasts everywhere, of all ages. It is for these new magicians that this catalogue was compiled. It's a guide to the wonderful world of modern magic. In it, we have included the best effects available from designers, manufacturers, and dealers in the materials of magic. What magic do you prefer—reading minds, sawing a body in two, card or coin tricks, or fabulous escapes? The secrets of the trade are available in these pages. Whether you are a novice or have been advancing your skills, you'll find both classic effects and the latest and most astounding variations, whatever suits your talents and inclinations.

Beginners will discover that not all magic must be done onstage to a large audience to baffle and entertain. Tricks with a deck of cards, a pair of dice, or coins can amuse and amaze an audience of one in the home, at the office, over lunch or dinner. Magic can make you more welcome at parties. It can help you to break the ice and meet new friends. Magic can truly add a deeper dimension to your life.

While many effects take commitment and practice to master, some of the most fascinating can be done instantly with equipment that works automatically and without detection. So what you find in this catalogue is variety to fit your interests and your skills. There are large stage illusions as well as small intimate tricks, classic tricks, and refinements of those classics. There are magic effects that must be practiced, practiced, and practiced more for perfection, as well as tricks that can be obtained inexpensively and performed immediately.

Whether magic is your hobby, a part-time vocation, or an all-consuming passion, you'll find something in this catalogue for you.

It's almost magical how magic has survived

the centuries. From prehistoric times when Stone Age men believed in magic and immortalized their sorcerers in cave drawings to this space-age century when trips to the moon are considered almost ordinary, we still react to magic with awe, joy, and excitement.

In every age, magic has survived. Magicians, real and imaginary, have achieved fame. Few people do not recognize the name of Merlin, the most famous magician in the history of English-speaking lands. The sixth-century Arthurian legend credits Merlin with the marvelous feat of transporting the giant stones of Stonehenge from Ireland to England, where they still stand.

Perhaps they came from Britain's "magic isle" of Man in the Irish Sea, where tales are still told of the wizard-king Manannan. His cloak changed color to make the sky blue, the sea green, or, in times of danger, the mists heavy and gray to hide the island from invaders. But the island's "perpetual fire" died, as did its wizard-king, and a race of giants came to Man, where they ruled until Merlin came upon the scene and vanquished them.

Like the natives of Man, almost every people remembers its ancient magicians. The North American Indian tribes still honor their tribal medicine man or the shaman who keeps alive the miraculous feats of his ancient predecessors.

Magicians and sorcerers were honored in the court of Egypt. One of the first magic shows ever recorded was given in Egypt before the Pharaoh Cheops about 3000 B.C. According to the translation of the Westcar papyrus now owned by the State Museum in East Berlin, a magician named Didi amused the court by rejoining the severed heads of an ox, a goose, and a pelican and by having a lion tamely follow him wherever he went.

Even the Bible records the feats of Egypt's magicians in Exodus, Chapter 7, which describes a contest between Moses and Aaron, who led the Israelites, and the sorcerers of the Pharaoh. In the Biblical account, the Lord bade Aaron "cast down his rod before Pharoah and his servants." The rod turned into a serpent, but the Pharaoh's sorcerers used their secret arts to do the same thing. The Lord's power conquered all as Aaron's rod swallowed up the snakes of the Egyptians. The rods-into-snakes tricks is part of the modern repertoire.

In the fabled lands of Tibet, Arabia, and the states of India, the stories of magical fakirs and lamas are still part of the lore. The tribes of Africa had their sorcerers, as did the ancient Greeks, those masters of logic and philosophy, and the noble Romans who conquered the ancient world. Throughout the Empire, the favorite performers were called *acetabularii*, from *acetabula*—"cups"—because they performed the feat known as "cups and balls." Centuries later the effect is still considered to be a great classic of magic. The "balls" used in Roman days were round white pebbles, making the trick more difficult to do than it is today, using light cork balls. The Greeks, too, had a version of the cups-and-balls routine, as early as 300 B.C. The skill of Eurybates of Oeschaelita at manipulating the cups and balls was so great that a statue was erected in his honor.

During the Dark Ages, jugglers and gypsies wandered through Europe carrying with them the inevitable cups and balls. As late as the year 1000 A.D., these wandering performers, known as *joueurs des gobelets*—goblet (cup) players—amused the courts of Europe. Rabelais, the great French writer who died in 1553, says of Panurge, one of his best-known characters, "He had little cups, wherewith he played very artificially."

The Birth of Hocus Pocus

A hundred years later the general term for a conjurer was a "hocus pocus," though there is some uncertainty about the precise origin of the term. One suggestion is that Ochus Bochus was the name of an old demon. Another is that "hocus pocus" is a corruption of *"Hoc est corpus,"* "This is [my] body," the Latin for Jesus' words at the Last Supper when initiating the sacramental transformation of bread and wine. Magicians—in fiction—often used those words when a magical transformation was to take place.

One of the earliest published guides to magic, *Hocus Pocus Junior,* appeared in 1634, with the frontispiece showing a magician of the day with his cups and balls in front of him. In 1640, a volume called *The Witts Recreations* was published in England containing these lines:

Here Hocus lyes, with his tricks and his knocs
Whom death has made sure as a juggler's box;
Who many have cozen'd by his legerdemain,
Is presto convey'd and here underlain.
Thus Hocus he's here, and here he is not,
While death played the Hocus, and brought him
   to th' spot.

"Legerdemain" is the word formally used to indicate magic that is performed with no reference to the occult. Stage illusions are an example. The word comes from the French *léger de main*, "light in the hand." The term "sleight of hand" may have come from that phrase also—a "sleight" is an unseen move made by a magician to add, subtract, move, or otherwise alter something secretly. A less innocent translation might be "light-fingered."

Of course it all suggests the common phrase "The hand is quicker than the eye," which may sound good, but simply isn't so. Saying it, though, diverts the attention of the audience and predisposes them to believe they could not see the magician's secret moves. The famed magician Robert Houdin, whom we will discuss further, used to send cards flying "invisibly" from one part of a pack, held by a spectator, to another part of the pack, held by another spectator, diverting their attention with talk. "When I tap with my wand, a card will fly through the air," he would say. "There, did you see them? I did, but possibly my eyes are faster than yours."

That's showmanship. And showmanship—the props and patter—is part of the act. Such discussion of the magic as it is being performed is helpful to the performer. Patter not only distracts the spectators, it keeps them amused. It also helps in "misdirection"—turning the spectator's attention elsewhere so he is not aware of the gadgetry or trickery taking place.

Even the stolid Germans succumbed to the delights of performance magic around 1800 with the advent of the *Taschenspieler,* or "pocket player." Using a bag or apron, German magicians were able to perform while surrounded by an audience. From these performances came the expressions "It's in the bag" and "He's exhausted all the tricks in his bag." At the same time the Italians were developing the same magical idea in the *bossoletino,* which literally means "purse man."

Famous Performers of the Eighteenth and Nineteenth Centuries

As the decades passed, magicians improved their skills and earned international reputations—even in the New World. Signor Antonio Blitz, born somewhere in Europe, died in Philadelphia in 1877. He was a magician and ventriloquist whose act was so popular in America that it is said he once had thirteen slavish imitators at the same time, all of whom used the same name, making his "personal appearances" very magical indeed.

Bartolommeo Bosco, born in 1790, is considered to have been the greatest magician in Italy; he raised the cups-and-balls routine to the level of art. Using three cups, each 3 inches high, placed upside down on a board or table, he would lift them one by one to show there was nothing underneath. Then, taking a cork ball in his right hand, he would transfer it to his left and order it to go underneath the cup. When his hand was opened, the ball would be gone and—yes!—there it would be under the cup. He would then make the ball vanish, appear and reappear under various other cups, and even change in size. The trick is still done today, essentially the same way as it was done originally.

Bosco had an adventurous life. He served under Napoleon, where he was wounded at the battle of Borodino fighting the Cossacks. It is claimed that he lay upon the ground as if dead, and when a looter came by picking pockets, Bosco managed to relieve the man of all his stolen goods as he rifled Bosco's "dead" body. Bosco is perhaps best known for having invented the card frame, a trick in which a spectator selects a card in secret only to have it mysteriously appear inside the glass and backing of a picture frame that has previously been taken apart in front of the audience and shown to be ordinary.

Isaac Fawkes, an outdoor performer at English street fairs, dominated English magic in the eighteenth century, accumulating a fortune of 10,000 pounds sterling by the time he died in 1731. His best-known effect was the egg bag, in which eggs appeared and disappeared mysteriously. Giuseppe Pinetti, an enormous sensation in Paris and throughout Europe, dominated the second half of the eighteenth century, but squandered his life savings on the then-new aeronautical fad of hot-air ballooning.

Phillippe, who began life as Jacques Talon, a French candymaker, gave a mystical air to his performances by dressing in Oriental costume. However, he also appeared with bare arms, in contrast to the many magicians who relied on flowing robes with baggy sleeves to hide things. Phillippe's great contributions were the introduction into the Western repertoire of several now-famous effects which include the linking rings, in which several hoops of metal are shown separately, magically linked together, passed to the spectators for examination, then unlinked. It is a trick so simple and direct that it is astounding. Phillippe also introduced the magical production of water with live goldfish.

The Scottish magician John Henry Anderson, born in 1814, began his professional career as an actor. Sir Walter Scott called Anderson the Wizard of the North, a name he adopted. Anderson gained and lost fortunes. He started newspapers, sold books on magic, built his own theaters, and gave masked balls. In 1849 he appeared before Queen Victoria and Prince Albert, then he went on to tour Australia, Hawaii, and the United States. "To sum up his history," wrote Houdini, "he stands unique in the annals of magic as a doer of daring things."

Like many magicians, Anderson was accused of being in league with the Devil on more than one occasion. He once was turned away from an inn by a landlord who told him, "Na, na, Mr. Anderson, or whatever else ya call yoursel'. I hae heard o' yer deevil's tricks and witcheries afore ye cam', and ye'll get nae lodgin' here." Anderson had to have the parish priest intercede for him before he could get supper and a bed.

The Birth of Modern Magic

Interesting and important as these early modern magicians were, the greatest impact on the magic of today was made by Jean-Eugene Robert, the nineteenth-century French magician who added his wife's maiden name to his and performed as Robert Houdin. Robert Houdin invented elaborate mechanical automatons, including one that could write the answers to questions. He also performed by clear light on an uncluttered stage and in formal evening attire, a revolutionary approach to magic.

By clearing the stage of obvious hiding places for assistants and by ruling out such forms of magical "skill" as having hidden assistants in the audience disguised as paying spectators, Robert Houdin earned the title "the father of modern magic." Two of the most popular effects developed by Robert Houdin, who worked with his son, were the aerial suspension, and a second-sight trick which was done by means of an elaborate and detailed code in which the choice of words used would convey everything.

Robert Houdin had the distinction of being called upon by the French government to put down with magic a rebellion in Algeria led by sorcerers. He convinced the rebels of his supernatural powers, challenging their strongman to lift a trunk. The man failed because a strong electromagnet under the platform where the trunk sat attracted the trunk's metal components and therefore the strongman could not lift it. He also asked a hostile member of the Arab group to fire a bullet at him. The young man was more than pleased to do so — but after Robert Houdin apparently caught the bullet in midair, there was only enough time for the youth to identify it positively as the one he had fired before the superstitious rebels fled in fear and panic. The bullet-catching trick has since been performed by many magicians, including Milbourne Christopher, who caught a bullet in his teeth on a national television show.

At the turn of the century, conjuring achieved its finest flowering. People thrilled to the magic of Herrmann the Great, Harry Kellar, Howard Thurston, and Blackstone. Full evenings of elegant magic were produced. The beautiful, baffling, and fabulous effects they invented or revised have become the legendary feats of today's magic.

While few modern magicians seriously claim that demons aid them, many performers found that a neatly trimmed beard like that of the traditional portrayals of Mephistopheles added a devilish appearance that was almost hypnotically effective in convincing people that they were seeing miracles. Alexander Herrmann made particularly effective use of his diabolic appearance during his tours of North and South America during the second half of the last century. His polished sleight-of-hand was legendary; he often performed impromptu on street corners wherever he happened to be. Known as Herrmann the Great, he was one of the most popular magicians in the world, and certainly the most famous seen in America up to that time.

There were other Americans. T. Nelson Downs, born in Marshalltown, Iowa, in 1867, worked as a railway telegrapher and spent hours playing with the money in the change drawer, developing remarkable skill at manipulation. He built a worldwide reputation as the "King of Koins," and was the first performer to specialize in coin magic.

Harry Kellar, born in 1849, was one of the world's classic illusionists. He rarely bothered with sleight-of-hand, carrying full evening shows on the strength of his incredible showmanship and impeccable attention to detail. When Kellar retired in 1908 his show was purchased by Howard Thurston, then thirty-nine years old. From then until his death in 1936, Thurston was in the top rank of American magicians.

Kellar and Herrmann had a great rivalry, exposing each other's tricks. Kellar's effects were generally more spectacular, but when Thurston took over from Kellar, the younger man was already establishing a reputation for his card handling. It didn't hurt that the great Kellar formally presented Thurston as his chosen successor during a performance in Baltimore. Thurston's most famous illusion was making an automobile vanish from midstage.

The Great Houdini

At the same time, young Erich Weiss was also appearing in America. Born in 1874, the son of a rabbi, Weiss traveled with circuses and carnivals before he was twenty. He adopted the name of his French idol, Robert Houdin, with some modification, and became world-famous as Houdini, a name he made synonymous with magical wizardry. His full-evening magic show aroused storms of applause everywhere. Houdini was able to make an elephant vanish, a legendary feat at the time.

Houdini was most famous for escapes, challenging members of the audience to put him into any kind of bondage or shackle. There is no record that he ever failed to escape. In one of his most spectacular escapes, he was bound and handcuffed and then put into stocks so that his feet were tightly imprisoned. The stocks were then raised above a large tank full of water and Houdini was lowered inside while the stocks were bolted into place. Nonetheless, he escaped, at the apparent peril of his life.

After Houdini's mother died he consulted many mediums and spiritualists to make contact with her, but without success. Sometimes a woman did speak to him "from spirit," but never speaking his mother's native Hungarian language. Finally, disgusted by the way in which fakes were preying upon the misery of their bereaved clients, Houdini launched a campaign to inform people how floating trumpets and other "spirit manifestations" were performed through trickery. One of the most popular forms these demonstrations took involved a seance with the participants blindfolded that took place in full light, so the audience could see.

Considered one of the greatest showmen in all of history, Houdini is honored even now by members of the International Brotherhood of Magicians, who make a pilgrimmage to his grave in Queens, N.Y., each Halloween, the anniversary of his death. There they perform a simple ceremony; a wand is broken at the exact minute he died, and everyone solemnly departs.

The Twentieth-Century Showmen

The last magician of the golden age of magic was Harry Blackstone, born Henri Bouton, in Chicago, in 1885. Blackstone effectively combined large illusions with smaller effects and sleight-of-hand. He died in California in 1965, but his son, Harry Blackstone Jr., continues performing the famous birdcage vanish and other tricks made famous by his father as well as inventing new ones. And there are many other young magicians carrying on in the great tradition, and whose work you will enjoy:

• Ricardo Suey—A South American magician who has made many television appearances in the United States.

• Absolon—A Czech who does a show of historical magic in Prague, acting out in highly dramatic form the burning of witches, etc.

• Chuck Jones—A California illusionist who

has seven people in his full-scale show of illusions.

• Maurice Fogel—A British mentalist who is surely the best since Dunninger. His act is insanely dangerous and completely unforgettable.

• Professor Zelpy—Some magicians produce doves; Zelpy dresses up like a dove and produces magicians. It's the most novel act in years.

• Frank Garcia—Probably the leading card and gambling authority in the world. Cheating and gambling magic, including cards and dice, is his specialty. And like John Scarne before him, he does great magic, too.

• Bev Bergeron—A comedy magic act for the whole family, a funny drunk in impeccable taste—and with incredible effects.

• David Copperfield—His magic introduced the 1978 ABC television shows and will be back to introduce ABC's lineup again in 1979. The young magician also sings and dances and is an all-around sensation.

• Charon—On the road fifty weeks a year, Charon is the last of a vanishing breed of performers in small-town auditoriums. With his wife, Judy, he does a show designed for the whole family.

• Milbourne Christopher—The author of many books on magic, Christopher is adept at large illusions and the close-up miracle. He is one of the best-known magicians in the world today.

There are perhaps a dozen more people who ought to be on this list, and in a few years' time, perhaps you, the reader, will be one of them. In that hope, and with that possibility clearly in view, this catalogue is dedicated to you.

# STAGE ILLUSIONS ON THE GRAND SCALE

Perhaps the most exciting, and mystifying, of all the magic effects has to do with the large stage illusions that are not just an act but a professional performance. Probably the most popular of stage illusions are those dealing with the severing of parts from the body, or those which enable a person to disappear.

It is impossible to write about stage illusions without mentioning Percy Thomas Tibbles, known as P.T. Selbit. A turn-of-the-century magician, he is the one credited with building the equipment that could saw an assistant into two pieces. Even today, this trick still remains one of the most fascinating and perplexing. Before Selbit perfected his equipment, the dissection of a person was generally accomplished by placing one person—before the show began—in a large box, and then the other person would be placed in the box while the show was in progress.

There are several newer methods that are simply improved versions of what Selbit accomplished during his days. Perhaps the most mesmerizing is the one popularized by Ricciardi, which he has billed as "the perfect illusion," and with justification. Using his wife as an assistant, Ricciardi takes a large buzz saw and visibly cuts her in half. He leaves the blade located deep within the body and then invites the audience up to within a few feet of her to inspect the situation. While it is obvious that the blood is merely colored sawdust, it is equally obvious that real ether was used in "drugging" the woman. However, it isn't obvious how it is possible for the blade to remain in her body. But remain it does, and Ricciardi achieves this illusion time after time, to the total amazement of his audience. (This is not to say that the illusion is not dangerous. Once, in fact, a piece of cloth from his wife's robe became caught in the whirling blade, and she actually was cut slightly.)

Other versions include decapitation and removal of arms and legs, wrists and fingers—which are all replaced in perfect condition before the illusion is terminated. These large stage effects do have an element of danger to them, and therefore are definitely not for the beginner. Misuse, or insufficient knowledge, could be a costly mistake. However, there are many built-in safety features.

Other kinds of illusions of continuing popularity are levitations, productions, and vanishings. These can be achieved singly or in combination. For example, a woman can be loaded into a large prop cannon and "fired" through a plate-glass sheet. She can then reappear in other places.

Probably the two modern illusions that have created the most attention wherever they are performed are the stacked boxes and zig-zag. In the former, a woman steps into a cabinet, which is divided into four boxes. These are stacked about the stage and then reassembled, but when the front doors are opened the woman is seen to have been assembled in the wrong order. Again the boxes are separated, rearranged, and stacked so that when the front is opened, she emerges whole once again.

In zig-zag a woman steps into a cabinet that reveals her face, hands, and feet. Then the center of the cabinet is pulled to one side so that she is forcibly disarranged. Her head and feet are in place, but her midsection—with one hand sticking out—is so far out of line that there is no apparent way she could actually be in one piece. In the hole obtained by sliding out that section, the magician can pass his hands to show there is nothing hidden.

Many large stage effects can be done with more modest equipment than would at first seem possible, and some can be built easily at home from workshop plans. For other effects, there are smaller versions, such as sawing a doll in two, that are quite interesting in performance, though they may well not operate by the same principles as the large illusions do.

For the large illusions as well as the small, the most effective element in providing an entertaining show is surprise. Never tell the audience what you are going to do before you do it, and never repeat an effect the same evening.

SAWING A LADY IN TWO

Here it is—the most famous illusion of all time. Everyone has seen pictures of it, cartoons of it, and so on, but few people have seen the real thing. And even after all these years, the real thing is stunning and beautiful to behold. This new version is even more incredible than ever, since the box and table are very small and leave no apparent room for concealment.

A woman is placed in a flat box resting on a thin table. Her head is sticking out of one end, and her feet are clearly visible coming out of the other end. Her feet and head are secured by stocks that slide down in metal grooves at each end of the box. She is solidly in place, and clearly visible at both ends.

Now the magician takes a large crosscut saw and begins to cut the box—and the woman inside—exactly in half, after which the two sections are separated and moved some distance apart. On Broadway, this was done and the feet section was wheeled offstage entirely.

In this version, only one woman is used, and the box can be put back together again for reuse later. So can the woman inside!

$1395

Lou Tannen
1540 Broadway
New York, N.Y. 10036

BUZZ SAW

It's all visible. A frame is shown onstage with a buzz saw hanging down over the middle of a girl who is strapped to a flat board. The big blade, powered by an electric motor, is turned on and the audience can hear its terrifying roar. The girl remains completely in view as the buzz saw descends and cuts slowly through her body.

No one who has seen this effect will ever be able to forget it. Especially when the girl later takes her bow, all in one piece.

$1725

Healey's Magic Co.
1612 Dickson Ave.
Scranton, Pa. 18509

MAKE-IT-YOURSELF AERIAL BROOM SUSPENSION

The performer's assistant steps on a small stool that has been placed in the center of a raised platform. The performer places two brooms or rods, one under each of her armpits. He then mesmerizes the assistant, and she slumps down, resting on the two brooms. The stool is removed, and the assistant remains suspended on the brooms. Now one of the brooms is removed and she still remains in the air. The performer now lifts her body slowly to a 45-degree angle and she stays suspended!

Lifting her until her body is horizontal to the floor, he leaves her levitated in this position, defying all the laws of nature and gravity! The procedure is now reversed, and the assistant is awakened to the resounding applause this effect always brings. Workshop plans.

$2

Warner's Magic Factory
Box 455
Hinsdale, Ill. 60521

SHREDDER

A table with four long legs is onstage. A large box, already in place, is on top of the table. The box consists of a flat board with holes in it. A board full of long spikes is attached above, and is lowered to show that they really do come out of the holes and stick several inches below the surface of the table. A girl lies down on the table, and her head and feet are clamped into place. Volunteers from the audience hold her head and feet. (The illusion may be performed surrounded.) Balloons are placed on the girl's body and the spiked board is lowered. The balloons burst, the spikes come out the bottom, and the audience is completely baffled. Naturally, when the board is removed the girl is unpunctured and smiling.

The spikes are solid steel. They do not bend or unscrew.

$900

Healey's Magic Co.
1612 Dickson Ave.
Scranton, Pa. 18509

MISPLACED LADY

A vertical cabinet is rolled onto the stage and a girl steps into it. The magician then takes six large blades and slides them into the cabinet at three locations, turning it into a stack of four boxes, separated from each other by the blades, which become the tops and bottoms of the boxes.

These boxes are then taken apart and placed onstage, then stacked back in place. The front of each box is opened like a door, and what is seen inside is the poor girl all scrambled up. Her head is next to the bottom box, underneath the one with her chest and shoulders in it, and so on. The doors are closed again, the boxes are restacked, and the girl walks out restored.

This is a startling effect, and has been performed hundreds of times on Broadway in the famous *Magic Show* that starred Doug Henning. It can be done surrounded, and on the floor or stage.

$1100

Healey's Magic Co.
1612 Dickson Ave.
Scranton, Pa. 18509

MAKE-IT-YOURSELF MECHANICAL CUT-OFF BUZZ-SAW ILLUSION

This modern up-to-date method of sawing a woman in half eliminates all thoughts of two girls being used or a trick box.

The magician's assistant is placed on a flat board and secured by shackles, under a motor-driven buzz saw suspended from a trestle. She remains in full view at all times. The motor is turned on, revolving with a wicked whine. Slowly the saw is swung over until it suddenly rips its way through the girl's body, severing the upper and lower parts. It's a weird and spine-tingling effect that leaves the audience gasping with horror and finally with relief when the girl is restored to life without bodily harm.

A sensational effect, and by an entirely safe and improved method that eliminates all hazard. Workshop plans and the complete secret are included.

$1

Warner's Magic Factory
Box 455
Hinsdale, Ill. 60521

IN-AGAIN, OUT-AGAIN

A large chest with a thin platform is shown. It is completely turned around. A girl steps into a sack and is placed in the chest. The top of the bag is passed through a hole in the lid and tied to a rod. The magician grasps the top of the sack and pulls it out. When the trunk is opened, the girl has vanished. Later, the girl appears.

$900

Healey's Magic Co.
1612 Dickson Ave.
Scranton, Pa. 18509

CANDLE THROUGH ARM

A fantastic illusion you can afford! A 10-inch metal cylinder is passed over the arm of volunteer assistant. A long flaming candle is pushed right through two holes in the center of the cylinder. The candle apparently goes through the arm!

The tube may be shown before and after. If you perform for audiences, you should have this!

$15

Magic and Fun
P.O. Box 1936
Grand Central Station
New York, N.Y. 10017

VOTA BATHTUB MYSTERY

This is a gigantic illusion that requires numerous assistants and is truly spectacular for a large show. The assistants set up a large platform and erect a skeleton framework of tubing on it. Cloth curtains are hung on the tubing and the curtains are closed. A gun is fired, the curtains are drawn back, and the interior of the cabinet is seen to have changed into a full bathroom, including a bathtub with a girl inside. Detailed notes on the presentation of this astonishing effect are provided along with the equipment.

$3000

Healey's Magic Co.
1612 Dickson Ave.
Scranton, Pa. 18509

WHITE CARGO CAGE

A gorgeous cage is seen onstage. A girl steps into the cage and is seen through the bars. The magician fires a shot and the girl vanishes. The cage is then taken apart in front of the audience. A sensational disappearance.

$875

Healey's Magic Co.
1612 Dickson Ave.
Scranton, Pa. 18509

LATTICE SCREEN MYSTERY

A girl stands on a platform and a lattice screen is placed around her to form a four-sided box. She can be plainly seen through the openings in the wooden slats that make up the screen. A pistol is fired and the screen tips over and falls flat on the stage. As the screen falls, the girl is seen to disappear.

$500

Healey's Magic Co.
1612 Dickson Ave.
Scranton, Pa. 18509

TABOURET CABINET ILLUSION

A beautifully decorated cabinet is shown. A girl climbs into the cage (there is no way she could be concealed in the steps) and curtains are lowered on all four sides of the cabinet. The magician signals to have the cage lifted into the air, then fires a gun at it. The curtains are dropped and the girl has vanished.

$800

Healey's Magic Co.
1612 Dickson Ave.
Scranton, Pa. 18509

THE ASRAH LEVITATION

Of all forms of floating a woman in the air, this may be the most popular. She lies on a table and the magician covers her with a cloth and waves his hand over her body, and she slowly rises into the air. The magician walks around her and underneath her as he continues to make motions in her direction. She can go up or down as he wishes. Then, as an alarming climax, he grabs the cloth and pulls it down. She has vanished! If desired, she can quickly reappear in the front of the theater.

$1000

Healey's Magic Co.
1612 Dickson Ave.
Scranton, Pa. 18509

PALANQUIN

An oblong box is rolled onstage on four long legs. It is turned to show both front and back. Curtains are then pulled open to reveal the box as

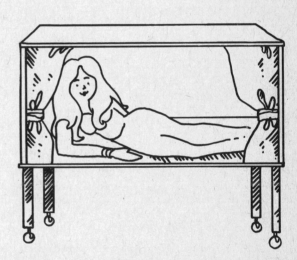

empty. The curtains are drawn. Suddenly a girl has appeared inside the box—from nowhere. This is a popular way to introduce your assistant.

$500

Healey's Magic Co.
1612 Dickson Ave.
Scranton, Pa. 18509

DAGGER CHEST ILLUSION

Here is something that looks wonderful, yet is easy to do.

A small box is placed over someone's head. Many daggers are thrust through the box repeatedly. The front panel of the box is removed, and inside are all the daggers, going every which way and filling up most of the box. There is no sign, however, of a head—damaged or otherwise.

The front cover is put back into place, and then one by one the daggers are removed. When the chest is lifted up, the assistant's head is back in its proper place—on her shoulders—and shows no signs of injury.

This folds flat and will fit into a suitcase, the trick is ready to do and easy to work. You get instructions, the head chest, and daggers.

$65

Dagger stand $9.50

Lou Tannen
1540 Broadway
New York, N.Y. 10036

PRINCESS FLYING CARPET

A small platform, on casters, is rolled to any spot on the floor that you wish. Resting on the platform is a beautifully designed screen that folds in half. The screen supports a platform with a gold fringe, which represents a flying carpet.

A young girl, weighing up to 140 pounds, sits crosslegged on the carpet. Two chrome swords are placed on the platform to further support the carpet. Now the screen is removed from the platform and set onto the floor away from the carpet. Then the swords are removed. These are waved over, under, and around the carpet as it stays suspended in midair.

Now the magician waves his wand toward the carpet, and it slowly revolves with the girl so that all four sides can be seen. A solid hoop can be passed over the girl and carpet and then taken away.

This is without question one of the finest and most baffling illusions ever devised, and it is based on a device made out of aluminum that

weighs only 5 pounds. The entire outfit packs flat for easy transportation. Everything is included but the girl and the hoop. Many people use a Hula Hoop for this purpose.

$137.50

Aladdin Magic Shop
110 S. High St.
Columbus, Ohio 43215

CANNON AND CRYSTAL BOX

The performer builds up a box of glass on the platform. A large hoop filled with paper is set up in front of the glass box, and on the other side of it is a large cannon. The magician's assistant is loaded into the cannon, which is aimed at the glass chest. The cannon is fired. There is a loud noise, a flash, a puff of smoke—and the paper is torn in the paper hoop. Inside the glass box the assistant is seen where she has "landed" safely.

Workshop plans.

$5

Lou Tannen
1540 Broadway
New York, N.Y. 10036

BELLY BUSTER

A tall cabinet is shown with an open front and back. It is about 5 feet high by 18 inches square, and can fold in half for packing. A large weight, 17 inches square, is shown to be solid. It is the type of weight used in gyms for lifting to the chest and over the head.

Two spectators come up to assist and hook the weight to the top of the chest. A girl placed on a board in the path of the weight would seem to be in a lot of danger if it were to fall on her. A balloon is placed above and below the girl's body. You explain that the idea is to lower the weight slowly so that it breaks the balloon, and then continues on down through the body and board to break the balloon underneath.

As you explain the idea of the trick, you actually demonstrate. The block is seen to penetrate the girl's body and the board, and goes on to break the bottom balloon. Since the platform is on casters, when the block is through the center of the girl you can turn the cabinet all the way around to show it completely through her body, front and back.

This incredible illusion can be performed close-up and surrounded! And yes, the block really does break the bottom balloon—nothing else does.

$350

Aladdin Magic Shop
110 S. High St.
Columbus, Ohio 43215

NEW FRENCH GUILLOTINE

This solid, realistic-looking guillotine stands almost 6 feet high. The large, heavy blade zooms

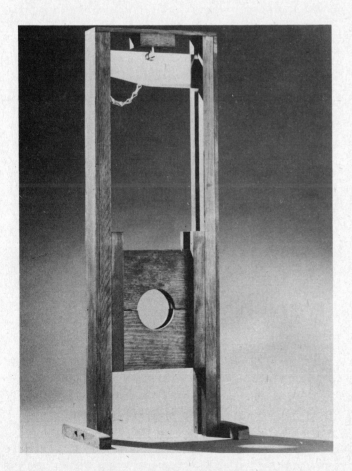

down clear through the neck stock and out the bottom, clear to the floor. The effect with this new model is really startling.

The equipment is very sturdy and looks dangerous, but folds very small for easy carrying and can be set up in two minutes. Quality construction.

$97.50

Lou Tannen
1540 Broadway
New York, N.Y. 10036

FRENCH ARM CHOPPER

One of the greatest inventors in modern magic, U.F. Grant, has come up with the new principle that is involved in this miniature guillotine. The spectator's hand actually falls off! You don't switch the hand—and you don't end up with any spare fingers after each performance.

Any spectator places his hand through the opening in this dangerous-looking little device. The large blade extending from each side of the chopper slowly descends. The arm is seen to fall off into a basket in front of the chopper. A riot ensues.

All part of a day's work for the magician. The whole operation is bloodless and the arm is safely restored. The blade does not slide or hinge, and can be used to chop carrots and the usual things as a demonstration of its effectiveness.

The chopper stands 2 feet high and is more than 1 foot wide.

$42.50

Lou Tannen
1540 Broadway
New York, N.Y. 10036

NEW CANVAS BOX ILLUSION

A box is built upon the stage by putting together six prefabricated panels—top, bottom, and four sides. These are merely wooden frames covered with heavy canvas on one side, which are thoroughly secured with heavy tacks all the way around. All of the panels can be inspected by audience members before they are put together.

The box is built around your assistant, who stands on the bottom panel as the others are put into place and secured with heavy straps placed crossways. She disappears instantly, or is changed into someone else, whichever you prefer. This is very baffling since the audience members themselves have inspected and built the box.

Price on request

Lou Tannen
1540 Broadway
New York, N.Y. 10036

ELECTRIC SAWING THROUGH THE NECK

This is a stunning portable illusion that can be done surrounded and fairly close to people. Not only that, no one will ever figure out how it is done, and it has all of the appearance of something that is insanely dangerous.

The "victim" kneels and puts his head in a set of stocks—actually a kind of pillory with a beautiful wood grain and trimmed with metal-flake glitter. This rests on a pair of chrome legs.

The "executioner" then brings out an electric Black & Decker saber saw and, as far as the spectators can tell, proceeds to cut right through the person's neck. The blade can be examined later; it gives no hint as to how this can be done.

If you work alone and want something exciting to do, this may be what you have been looking for. Just think of the activity that would be caused by trying to get a volunteer from the audience for this! And yet there is not the slightest bit of danger.

$150

Lou Tannen
1540 Broadway
New York, N.Y. 10036

ZIG-ZAG ILLUSION

This illusion can be done under any and all conditions. It can be watched from any angle without detection. And it is very, very baffling.

The effect is that your assistant walks into a vertical cabinet that is wheeled in on casters. The feet are seen at the bottom and a face is seen at the top. Hands appear with handkerchiefs or silks in them. And then the middle is taken out to one side where it could not possibly be.

$1195

Lou Tannen
1540 Broadway
New York, N.Y. 10036

CANE TO LIT CANDLE

Here's an impressive way to fire up any audience and keep them begging for more. This is no ordinary cane feat but something special. At any time during your act, pick up your steel vanishing cane, make it disappear, and replace it with a 13-inch *lit* candle.

This trick has proved to have a spellbinding opening effect, since it appears to be impossible that you could have made the cane vanish and replaced it with the candle. The trick is so realistic that you're likely to stump fellow magicians. And you're sure to be the envy of others as they tire of the same old cane-to-silks routine. It's brand-new, completely automatic, and fully guaranteed in workmanship. Remember, the candle comes out of the cane lit! (You can use your own cane.)

Electronic candle from cane $24.50 postpaid
Steel vanishing cane $24.50 postpaid
Set (cane & electronic candle) $45 postpaid

Theater Effects, Inc.
P.O. Box 293
South Bound Brook, N.J. 08880

ARM CHOPPER GUILLOTINE

Scary, but entirely safe. Blade looks as though it will slice through spectator's wrist—but of course it won't! Crafted from selected woods with a stainless-steel blade. Stands almost 30 inches high.

$35 plus postage

Zanadu
165 Hancock Ave.
Jersey City, N.J. 07307

TRIPLE FLORAL CYLINDERS

The performer begins the effect by freely showing three empty chromed cylinders. *Please bear in mind that the cylinders are freely shown.* Three pots of roses are produced from the cylinders in rapid succession. The roses are natural-looking; each pot of roses is a different color of feather flowers. The three chromed cylinders are embossed in design and trimmed in bright red. Each pot of roses is 18 inches high and contains twelve blooms (thirty-six in all). Everything is stage-size and made of the best materials money can buy. No hooks or other outdated methods are used; the effect is entirely self-contained, entirely new in design, and very easy to do.

This beautiful effect is always ready to use and can be the feature of your show—full professional size, and yet it packs small. Complete with three chromed cylinders, three elegant pots of roses, and complete detailed instructions.

$250

H. Marshall & Co.
294 W. South St.
Akron, Ohio 44311

GIANT COLOR-CHANGING APPLAUSE CARD

A huge, 11×17-inch card reading "Applause Please" in black bold letters is shown at the appropriate moment. After the reaction, the card is turned over; and, in large green letters, the audience reads, "Thank You." Then the card is turned over once more, and instead of the expected "Applause Please," the spectators see a hilarious gag line in bright-red letters.

A funny gag, a great trick, and a surefire applause getter all rolled into one.

$5

Jacobs Productions
Box 362
Pomeroy, Ohio 45769

LIGHTER-THAN-AIR LEVITATION

Every stage show requires at least one girl that floats through the air. Here it is!

No back drop is required, and no assistant; the magician may set up and perform the trick alone, onstage, in a parlor, or at a lawn party.

The magician can walk completely around girl while she is floating. Any girl from the audience may be used. The girl rises to a height of 6 feet above the floor, and a solid hoop is passed over her entire length. The magician controls every movement of this spellbinding illusion, which may be transported in the back seat of an automobile.

$1645

Phil Moore
G. H. Grimm Co.
Rutland, Vt. 05701

THE GIRL AMONG THE FLOWERS

This illusion, as the audience first sees it, is a background, set against curtains about 10 feet long and 8 feet high, representing a mass of flowers and bushes mixed together with a blue sky above. There is a flat roof projecting out about 3 feet from the bottom of the screen, supported by four poles set at equal distances. This divides the background in three equal parts. The floor is raised about a foot from the stage, and this also is divided in three equal panels with electric lights in each panel to set off this improvised greenhouse. The spectators are satisfied that there is no deception, for they can see all there is to see.

In presentation, a semicircular stand is placed in front of the middle panel at the height of the floor. At the roof is a rod in the form of a semicircle, from which hangs a curtain enclosing the little stand. The audience is still satisfied there is no deception, as they can still see behind the curtain, on the extreme right and left.

In a moment the curtain is withdrawn and a beautiful girl surrounded by flowers is seen standing on the little platform.

A very convincing and mystifying illusion. Adds beauty to any stage performance.

$2000

Healey's Magic Co.
1612 Dickson Ave.
Scranton, Pa. 18509

MURDER IN THE TELEPHONE BOOTH

A cabinet is shown onstage to appear as a telephone booth. A young girl comes running onstage in great fright. She sees the telephone booth, runs inside, and calls up on the phone for help. A madman is pursuing her. The madman stealthily enters with a huge knife, sees the girl at the phone, sneaks up, opens the door a trifle, raises his arm, strikes. The girl screams and falls. Naturally, the madman escapes.

A boy from the audience runs up onstage all excited, opens the phone-booth door, and runs frightened offstage. A policeman enters, sees the booth, approaches suspiciously, and opens the door wide. The booth is empty. He goes in, opens the rear door, and passes entirely through the cabinet. Nothing there. The policeman then removes his disguise and proves to be the girl! A sensational illusion which can last for five minutes.

$900

Healey's Magic Co.
1612 Dickson Ave.
Scranton, Pa. 18509

FLASH PAPER

A flash of fire at your finger tips—what better way to say that you're a magician? With this safe, chemically treated paper you can produce a bright yellow flash whenever you want. Flash paper will burn at very low temperatures, so it can be ignited with a match, candle, or cigarette. It burns very quickly, leaving no ash, and leaving everyone agape. Flash paper is sold in two forms: a small pad, about 2×3 inches, containing twenty sheets; or large sheets, 8×10 inches, four to an envelope. Flash paper is easy to use and amazing to watch and it's a great way to call attention to yourself anywhere! Because flash paper does produce fire it cannot be sold to people under sixteen years of age.

Pad $1.25
Envelopes $2

The Wizard
1136 Pearl St.
Boulder, Colo. 80302

MAGIC FLOWERS

Along with producing rabbits and silks, flowers are a great production number. The huge blooms are easily concealed but produce ohs and ahs from the audience. Puts real color in your act.

Five-bloom bouquet $32.50
Eighteen-bloom bouquet $125

Dehoff's Florist
Rt. 6, Box 661, Bankert Rd.
Hanover, Pa. 17331

CHIPS-N-SIPS

The magician breaks the seal on a fresh can of ordinary potato chips. He pours and serves some, covering the remaining chips and can with a decorative chrome canister. When the canister is removed, the potato chips are changed into a can of beer or soda pop. This may also be opened and served.

If soda pop, five different flavors may also be poured from the same can. These flavors may be served to members of the audience.

With two of these chrome canisters you can make the pop and potato chips change places, finally ending with two cans of pop, no potato chips, and sponge balls, sponge sandwich, or some other similar sponge load as a final production.

Price includes one chrome-plated canister, ten "Dingles" labels to make the ordinary potato chips into magic chips, and full instructions. You provide the edibles.

$10.50

Klamm, the Magic Man
1412 Appleton
Independence, Mo. 64052

THE DOLL HOUSE

A small doll house is sitting onstage. The front doors are opened and the house is seen to be empty. A doll is placed in the house and the doors are shut. The house is revolved, and the top bursts open, followed by a girl that fills the house.

$395

Deratzian Magical Enterprises
922 Spring Ave.
Troy, N.Y. 12180

SHACKLE ESCAPE

A large box has a board suspended by chains. The plank floats on chains in full view of the audience. The front of the box has curtains which hang below the plank. The assistant lies on the plank and his ankles and wrists are manacled and locked to the board. His neck is locked in a steel collar and also locked to the board. The spectator may furnish his own locks. The curtains are closed, and upon opening, the assistant has vanished.

$850

Healey's Magic Co.
1612 Dickson Ave.
Scranton, Pa. 18509

LIGHTED BOX MYSTERY

A paper-covered wooden-framed box is shown onstage. The magician opens the front door and steps inside, moving a light bulb around inside of the cabinet. He steps out, closes the door, and swings the bulb around each side to show light through paper, proving nothing is concealed behind any wall. He places the bulb inside through a hole in the top. Soon mysterious shadows of hands, etc., appear on the paper, and finally a clear shadow silhouette of a girl materializes. She bursts through the paper of the front door, having magically materialized. One of the most baffling and beautiful ways to produce a person.

$1000

Healey's Magic Co.
1612 Dickson Ave.
Scranton, Pa. 18509

TWO-HOLE WRIST CHOPPER

This unusual chopper looks big, beautiful, and showy onstage, yet it works easily. It is made of hardwoods with a light walnut stain. The mir-

ror-bright blade has two 4-inch holes in it. Carrots may be placed in the matching holes of the chopper frame and cut with the blade. The blade is lifted and an assistant's hands are placed through the frame. Tie the wrists together or use handcuffs. The blade is pushed down, penetrating the wrists. But wait! The frame is then broken apart, revealing the blade with the assistant's wrists locked through the holes. Lift the blade and arms out, leaving only the bare skeleton of the chopper frame. Complete with fitted carrying case.

$195 postpaid

Delben Co.
P.O. Box 3535
Springfield, Mo. 65804

WIZARD WHIZ-BANG

If you want the audience looking in the wrong place while you maneuver a trick, you need this—the perfect climax to your act. Fires a .22 caliber blank cartridge with smooth, silent hair-trigger spring-loaded action. Machined in black anodized aluminum with turned steel tips. Firing pin is rimfire design for surefire operation every time.

$97.50

Cler'mont Specialties
26 S. Garden Ave.
Clearwater, Fla. 33515

FRENCH GUILLOTINE

This guillotine stands over 6 feet tall and looks truly dangerous. It is a wicked, gleaming beauty made out of solid mahogany and birch. The blade is stainless steel with a special finish designed to give the illusion of hollow-ground sharpness. A fitted carrying case is provided for protection and to make it easy for you to set up and repack this apparatus.

The effect is simply that someone puts his head in the slot and the blade falls. Unlike the days of the French Revolution, the victim's head remains intact, and properly attached. The blade moves down with realistic continuity from the top, through the head stock, and out the bottom. If you are looking for one big effect that will give chills and thrills, this is it.

$398

Delben Co.
P.O. Box 3535
Springfield, Mo. 65804

WIZARD SMOKE

Magicians are always looking for a reliable source of smoke for special effects. The same is true for people involved in theatrical productions and films. Wizard smoke is the real thing—and ready to use instantly. This chemical smoke, used in the past for skywriting, has been diluted for safe use by performers and stage technicians. It is packaged in a screw-top test tube in liquid form. When it is exposed to the air it produces real smoke. It may be used for close-up, or onstage; it's also great for haunted houses and seances. A little goes a long way, and its shelf life is well over a year. This is the only substance easily available that produces real smoke, as you need it.

$5

The Wizard
1136 Pearl St.
Boulder, Colo. 80302

BRITE-LITE FLOATING SKULL

In the dark it glows with spectacular brilliance! In the light it has real personality! Plays peek-a-boo, rock-a-bye baby; does the hula, gets the hiccups. Vents will love it! Throw your voice under the cloth while skull floats.

Handsome 7-inch skull is almost life-size, beautifully designed to look realistic. Features weirdly changing light pattern which makes skull seem to writhe into life. Use 36-inch or larger foulard, thanks to new, oversized flotation gimmick.

No batteries, yet entire skull glows with weird green brilliance. Not only is this skull bigger than any other floating skull—it's also much brighter than any other zombie-like effect, and costs less, too! So bright that in the dark it actually lights your hands and face, without revealing the gimmick! Lets you float it alone—completely uncovered—almost to the front row! Self-contained light gimmick.

The price includes skull plus lighting pack with sufficient energy for up to eight shows. Additional lighting packs are available. Complete instructions give suggestions for comedy and seasonal shows (such as Christmas, birthdays).

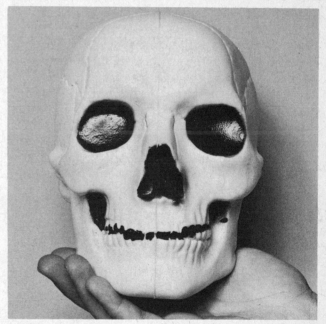

$19.50

Klamm, the Magic Man
1412 Appleton
Independence, Mo. 64052

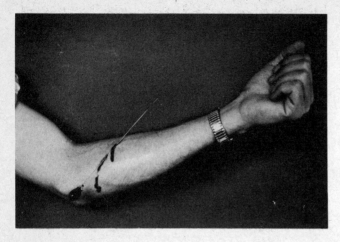

YOU-DO VOODOO

This is a method of duplicating the flesh-piercing feats of genuine voodooists and hypnotists. The only difference is that there is no actual injury to the performer. If you're looking for a great new trick to add to your kid show, then this is definitely not it! If instead you need a real convincer for a pseudo-hypnosis routine, or if you need a special lobby stunt to promote a voodoo theme or motion picture, or you just want to throw your family physician a real curve, then it is for you.

The effect: The magician, while discussing the rituals of voodoo, cleanses his arm with alcohol. He then sterilizes a 6-inch hat pin and thrusts it through his arm. He displays the punctured and bleeding wound at close range to his audience, removes the pin, and replaces it with a large threaded sewing needle. This is pulled back and forth through his arm, by a spectator, if he wishes, and then it is ripped out. The arm is then cleaned and there is no evidence of any damage whatsoever. This trick is not for the fainthearted.

$20

The Wizard
1136 Pearl St.
Boulder, Colo. 80302

FINGER CHOPPER

Wooden stocks with a stainless-steel blade riveted between them are shown. Any object placed beneath the blade may be severed in half—yet the performer is able to pass this blade harmlessly through his or a volunteer's finger!

The wooden stocks with the blade and the casing into which they nest are two separate pieces. Each piece may be minutely examined by the spectators both before and after the effect. The apparatus supplied is entirely of wood and metal construction, lacquer-finished with a natural tone. Each device is thoroughly inspected for precision and smoothness of operation before it is sold.

The illusion carries a dynamic impact and is equally effective when performed at a distance or close-up.

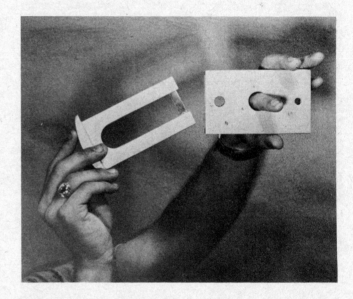

$15

Micky Hades International
Box 2242
Seattle, Wash. 98111

THE AERIAL BROOM SUSPENSION

Your assistant steps onto a small stool that has been placed in the center of a small raised platform. You place two brooms, one under each of her armpits. You hypnotize the assistant, and she slumps down and is supported by the two brooms. As she lies there in heavy sleep the stool is taken away and then one of the brooms is taken away also.

The audience is treated to the eerie sight of a woman clearly not touching anything at all except that broom, and yet suspended in air. This gets even more baffling when you grasp her feet and lift her slowly to a 45-degree angle, where she continues to rest upon a cushion of solid air and broomstraws.

Lifting her even further, you conclude with her body lying horizontally in defiance of gravity. Then the procedure is reversed, and she is awakened once more with her feet on terra firma. This is one of the most clean-cut and spectacular of all forms of levitation, and one of the most appreciated by audiences. Tony Curtis did a version of it in the film that he made about Harry Houdini many years ago.

$1050

Lou Tannen
1540 Broadway
New York, N.Y. 10036

3 CONJURING WITH CARDS

Probably no area of magic is as fascinating to an audience as the "miracles" done with an ordinary (or not so ordinary) deck of playing cards. The deck is fifty-two props divided into two colors and four suits, each suit with thirteen values. Think how those props can be juggled; how many magical possibilities they can provide! Think how an audience that has grown up playing card games from Old Maid to Twenty-one can be amused and amazed by what the cards can be made to do!

There are card tricks, completely automatic and self-working, that can be done by novices. The instructions are easy to follow; the steps are always the same; the result can be guaranteed. Cards can be made to appear and disappear; change from one value and suit to another. Red cards can be changed into black ones and a "regular" deck of cards can be transformed into a deck with fifty-two of a card in any color or value or suit.

The more dexterous the handling of the cards, the more amazing the tricks—sometimes with mechanical devices, often without. A magician can make a selected card rise mysteriously from a closed pack of cards and reappear in a balloon, underwater, in a spectator's pocket, or on the ceiling. A card can be torn, defaced, and then restored. A card trick can amaze an audience of hundreds or astonish your best friends at a party. There are hundreds of tricks to be mastered, so you can always come up with some new feat to excite and entertain.

Perhaps the greatest modern master of card sleights is John Scarne, who has perfected his art so that it truly seems magical. Having reached that pinnacle, he is willing to share his magic and has written books explaining hundreds of techniques that will help the novice or less skilled performer perfect his individual abilities. Scarne's autobiography is also entertaining and worth reading for its glimpse into a life built on cards.

Whether your goal is to become a professional magician or just to be a welcome guest at any party, proficiency comes with practice. And with practice you can make cards do almost anything.

ULTRA MENTAL DECK

This famous deck has taken its place among the classics of card magic. One of the effects is to place the full deck of cards on the table and state that you reversed *one* card in that deck. Have a spectator name *any* card. Pick up the cards, fan them, faces up, and you finally come to one card and one card *only* that is reversed. This proves to be the card named by the spectator! Remember, the spectator has a free choice and may name any one of the fifty-two cards in the deck, and that is the only card which is found to be reversed. Complete with deck and instructions for several other unusual effects.

$3

Warner's Magic Factory
Box 455
Hinsdale, Ill. 60521

THE BRAIN WAVE DECK

Truly a modern miracle! The performer places a deck of cards on the table and states that before leaving home, he removed one card from another deck and placed it face up in this deck. He asks a spectator to name a card—*any card*! The performer removes cards from case and runs through them until he locates the one face-up card. You guessed it! The card named by the spectator is the only face-up card, and its back is a different color than the rest of the deck!

$3

Warner's Magic Factory
Box 455
Hinsdale, Ill. 60521

SVENGALI MAGIC DECK

This is the wonder deck of magic! Instructions are included for ten different amazing tricks. With the Svengali deck you can predict *in advance* the card that a spectator will select, although you first prove that the cards are all different. You do not see or touch the selected card; still, you know its name. This is the easiest way to secretly "force" a spectator to choose the card you want. No skill required.

$1.50

Warner's Magic Factory
Box 455
Hinsdale, Ill. 60521

"OUT OF THIS WORLD"—PAUL CURRY

A poll of magicians called this the best of all card tricks—and with good reason. It is as simple and clear-cut a miracle as you could want.

Entirely unaided, a spectator deals a complete deck of cards face down into two piles, placing what he guesses are reds in one pile and blacks in the other—red or black purely a hunch. Several cards may be placed in the same heap one right after the other. Any suspicion of prearrangement is killed by the freedom allowed. Believe it or not, when the cards are turned over, one pile is all red, the other is all black.

And it's so very, very simple that anyone can do it. New improved instructions with various routines and subtleties.

$1

Flosso Hornmann
304 W. 34th St.
New York, N.Y. 10001

MARKED CARDS

Most common brands of playing cards are available marked for number and suit. You can read the backs as well as the fronts. This is great for a number of card tricks or for an exposé of gambler's tricks. These are sold for magical purposes only.

$5

Warner's Magic Factory
Box 455
Hinsdale, Ill. 60521

PENETRATION FRAME

This is a magical classic, and a real baffler. A clear sheet of plastic is mounted on a frame that can be critically examined both before and after the trick.

Two playing cards are inserted, one on each side of the frame, and held in place by clips which are a part of the frame. The magician then thrusts a pencil or other sharp pointed object right through the center of the cards and the solid plastic sheet. The cards are removed and examination of the plastic fails to reveal the sign of any hole.

$3.50

James Rainho Products
14 Windsor Rd.
Medford, Mass. 02155

TIME OUT

You show four cards: three blanks and one with the face of a clock printed on it. Put the clock card face down on the table and place the blank cards behind your back. Tap the card on the table and it turns blank. The clock card is found behind the back. Repeat the effect, using just two blank cards, with the same results. Finally offer to do it with just one blank card and the clock card. This time have the spectator tap the clock card on the table . . . whoops, it seems he tapped too hard and he broke the clock. The card now shows a busted clock. No hard moves, easy to do. Cards can be examined.

$2.50

James Rainho Products
14 Windsor Rd.
Medford, Mass. 02155

CHROMA CRAZY

The magician spreads out a deck of cards, showing both faces and backs. While the deck is face down a spectator is invited to select a card. Just as the spectator is about to make his selection, the magician closes up the deck, saying: "I'd better not do this trick. You see, I was up rather late last night, or should I say, I was still up rather early this morning. I went to a party and there was a lot of booze flowing around and I'm still a little woosy. I'm not saying that I'm drunk, I'm just suffering from bottle fatigue. You see, I have a legitimate reason for drinking. Last year I donated my body to science, so I'm preserving it in alcohol till they use it. Anyway, when I picked up the cards this morning, strange things

happened. You've heard of pink elephants? Well, I saw yellow spades. See, see what I mean . . ."

As the magician spreads the deck it is seen to contain only yellow spades. Suddenly it changes to all purple hearts, then to all green diamonds, and then to all red clubs. Finally the cards return to normal and the magician decides to try the trick anyway. The deck is fanned out, face down, and a spectator is told to remove a card but not to look at it yet. The magician then states that if he fails to name the selected card he will pay the spectator a dollar for every spot the selected card represents—a dollar for an ace, seven dollars for a seven, etc. The magician concentrates and names a card. The spectator looks at his selected card and the magician instantly comments, "I'm wrong, huh? Oh well, how much do I owe you?" This always provokes laughter because the spectator is holding a blank card. An entertaining routine that you will enjoy.

$8

James Rainho Products
14 Windsor Rd.
Medford, Mass. 02155

VOODOO RITE

Voodoo . . . the practice of magic rites prevalent in the West Indies, particularly Haiti, and in the southern United States.

Originally stemming from ophiolatry transmitted from African Ashanti cults, voodoo is characterized by erotic and symbolic dance rhythms. Occult chants and sacrifices of goats and chickens are other features of voodoo ritual. As late as the first decades of this century it involved human sacrifice and cannibalism.

Recreate this weird rite that always leaves people spellbound. The lights are dimmed and a candle burns on the table. A deck of cards is spread out and openly shown, faces and backs. It is then placed in the center of the table. A deck of small playing cards is introduced and two cards are selected from this deck. The two selected cards are placed, face up, on the table. The small cards represent voodoo dolls, or effigies, of the duplicates in the larger deck of cards.

A voodoo ritual is then conducted, inflicting curses on the "victims." The two curses are "death" by fire and by a deadly potion.

A match and a vial of liquid are shown. A spectator places the match on one of the small cards and the vial on the other—he has an absolutely free choice. The match is burned over the card it was placed on, and the liquid is rubbed on the card the vial was placed on. Now the larger deck of cards is picked up and spread out. Lo and behold! The curses have been successful! The duplicate of the card the match was burned over has a large hole burned in its center. The card that the potion was rubbed on has a stained face. The deck can be examined, as there are no duplicates. A curse-breaking finale is supplied where the "victims" are restored to their original condition. This is white magic with a black-magic theme.

$6.50

James Rainho Products
14 Windsor Rd.
Medford, Mass. 02155

PRIVATE EYE

An astounding effect with all the essentials to make it a dynamic masterpiece. It mystifies, it amuses, it entertains, and it's easy to do.

You can start by borrowing a deck of cards and having a card (any card) selected. The selected card is returned to absolutely anywhere in the deck. You then introduce a card with an eye printed on it and call it your "private eye" detective card. You state that you are getting too lazy to go looking for selected cards so you use a private eye to do it for you. The eye card is placed on top of the deck, and you tap it with your finger. You pick up the card, turn it over, and the eye has vanished from the card. The entire deck is spread out and the eye is found on the face of the selected card.

No phony moves. No card control. The special eye card can be examined.

$2.50

James Rainho Products
14 Windsor Rd.
Medford, Mass. 02155

SPLIT DECK

One of the most unusual card decks ever created. This special deck is actually cut in half diagonally. Get two spectators to assist. Pick up one half of the deck and show faces of cards to be all different, and have a half-card selected from this half. Show the other half and have the second spectator also select a half-card from the second half. When both half-cards are placed together they form a complete card, face and back. Unbelievable but true.

$2.50

Warner's Magic Factory
Box 455
Hinsdale, Ill. 60521

SYMBOL FORCE DECK

A specially designed deck of cards that will force the spectator to pick a design. The deck consists of various designs, symbols, etc. The "force" design is the treble clef used in music.

Show the cards to be all different, turn them face down, and have a spectator merely point to any card. That card will be the force card. This can be used to make predictions, etc. A must for every mentalist!

$3

James Rainho Products
14 Windsor Rd.
Medford, Mass. 02155

THE DATING GAME

These delightful, specially printed cards allow three hilarious tricks to be performed.

1.—The all-American boy (demonstrated with three specially printed cards). The sweet innocence of youth is demonstrated until he discovers the opposite sex—and the girl next door. He attempts to get her into compromising situations, which she always eludes. He finally traps himself as the last card indicates.

2.—Blind date (using six cards—five pretty girls and one ugly girl). The five cards with the pretty girls are shown and the one card with the ugly girl is inserted somewhere into the stack. The cards are cut several times according to a spectator's wishes. The spectator then makes a selection of a card . . . he always gets the ugly girl.

3.—The pick-up (shown with three special cards). Magician tells how he won a huge quantity of money in a poker game and then decided to go out and celebrate. He picked up a young lady at a local lounge and after a few drinks found himself in a motel—but the next thing that he knew it was morning and he found that all his money was gone and so was the young lady. All he got was the proverbial ROYAL _____.

Three entertaining effects, each with its own individual special cards. *The printing on the cards is not off-color.* The suggested stories are provided word by word. They are not X-rated.

$5

James Rainho Products
14 Windsor Rd.
Medford, Mass. 02155

ROAD RUNNER CARD TRICK

A trick you'll have fun with! You hold a packet of five cards. Top card, the Road Runner, is shown and placed on bottom. *"Beep beep"*—and he appears on top! This is done again, and he's back on top! Now the Road Runner is placed aside face down on table, but again he appears back on top of the packet! Everyone suspects more than one Road Runner, and sure enough four Road Runners are shown—but wait: *"Beep beep beep"*—and *all four vanish,* leaving blank cards! What made them disappear? The card laid aside is turned up and it's changed to that sly, old rascal Wile E. Coyote! Easy to do!

$2.50

Nick Trost Magic
1382 Virginia Ave.
Columbus, Ohio 43212

TRIPLE METAMORPHOSIS

Spread three cards and show them to be alike. Square up the cards into a stack and spread them again. One card has changed to a different card. Square and spread the cards again until all three have changed to the different card. Show the backs, and then change them also.

This lovely card routine is easy to do. You get the cards, instructions, and a full routine.

$2

Jose's Studio
17-C Wallace St.
Belleville, N.J. 07109

LAST GAME

Here is a card trick that has a funny story line and a few surprises that your audience will love. You show a weak five-card poker hand, which changes into five of a kind. Since that is one too many cards, the gambler was shot! All the backs instantly change to a floral pattern so that the flowers can be placed on the gambler's grave.

No special card-handling ability is required. This is self-contained and easy to do.

$3.50

Jose's Studio
17-C Wallace St.
Belleville, N.J. 07109

JUMPING JACK CARD

There is a giant-size card frame on the stage with a 6½×10-inch jack of hearts in it. The card vanishes in full view of everyone and is found on an easel behind a display card that has already been shown.

$48

Delben Co.
P.O. Box 3535
Springfield, Mo. 65804

FAN-KOTE

This useful item is for those who are interested in card magic in a serious way. It is used to put a very thin coat of fanning powder on cards, as if you had polished it on by hand. No loose residue is left on the card as it is withdrawn. The powder is used to make cards fan better, so that if you reach behind someone's ear to brush off a fan of cards that has gotten stuck there, you are sure the fan will open immediately and in the way you want it to open.

$7.50
Fanning powder $2.00

Delben Co.
P.O. Box 3535
Springfield, Mo. 65804

PAVLOV'S BELL

The magician shows a small box with a button that rings a bell inside the box when the button is pushed. He then tells a story about the famous Russian scientist who conditioned the behavior of dogs by ringing a bell. However, a strange thing happened. Instead of training dogs, the scientist somehow trained the bell—so that it would ring whenever a dog was near.

Five cards are shown, each with the picture of an animal on it. These are placed face down on a table. The magician—or a spectator—then holds the box without touching the button, and passes it over the cards. The bell rings by itself whenever it passes over the card that has the picture of a dog on it. This will mystify the audience, and comes complete with everything needed.

$15

Healey's Magic Co.
1612 Dickson Ave.
Scranton, Pa. 18509

ASTROLOGIC, THE ZODIAC CARD MIRACLE

On the table of a darkened room lies a zodiac chart, clearly picturing each of the twelve astrological symbols. From a shuffled deck of playing cards, twelve are dealt around the zodiac chart.

A spectator is invited to remove any number of cards from the chart and place them in his pocket. Gathering up the remainder of the cards, he notes and remembers one of them before replacing the packet on the balance of the deck.

All of the preceding is done while the performer's back is turned. Yet even so, he is at once able to give a detailed astrological reading for the spectator, reveal the number of cards hidden in his pocket, and perceive the card he merely peeked at!

The effect is done without the use of fake cards, confederates, or gimmicks of any kind. It is a perfect blend of mental card magic with the occult. It comes to you complete with everything you need, including cards, zodiac chart, detailed horoscopes for every sign, and full instructions.

$7.50

Micky Hades International
Box 2242
Seattle, Wash. 98111

CARD MAGIC

Be the magician you always wanted to be. Professional card magic kit includes two trick decks of cards, miracle card case, and two illustrated books on card magic. Master 225 easy-to-perform card miracles. Designed by professional magicians.

$6.50

Fun, Inc.
2434 N. Greenview Ave.
Chicago, Ill. 80614

THE CURSE OF DRACULA

The magician tells the legend of the vampire and shows four specially printed cards with the picture of a girl on each. Then he shows card with the picture of Count Dracula himself on it. The girls are merely touched by this card and change into vampire women. A wooden stake is thrust through their hearts and through the heart of Dracula himself. All cards now change to skeletons, and on the stake there is—*vampire blood!* Finally, a disturbing message appears, and for an extra surprise a black vampire bat appears and flits into the air.

This is a sensational collection of surprises, and it is also easy to perform.

$5

Glenn Comar
353 E. Sixth Ave.
Roselle, N.J. 07203

SEVENTH SIGHT

A pack of cards is handed out in bunches to a number of people so the performer is left with just a few cards in his hands. Each spectator is asked to think of any one of the cards he is holding. They are then shuffled together. One at a time the magician proceeds to discover the cards that were thought about. No sleight-of-hand. Nothing to memorize or learn. Detailed instructions and all the little devices necessary are supplied.

$5

Glenn Comar
353 E. Sixth Ave.
Roselle, N.J. 07203

THE LUCK OF LUCRETIA

A fascinating plot is incorporated into this great pocket trick. Six cards are shown, each with pictures of glasses of wine. One of the glasses has a large skull-and-crossbones symbol on it to show that it is poisoned.

"Have you ever heard of Lucretia Borgia?" you ask. "Every time she threw a party, one of the guests left the house in a coffin! She was an expert poisoner, and no matter how many guests were there or how many glasses, the right person always received the poison glass."

A spectator is invited to play the part of the victim. No matter how hard he tries to avoid the poison glass, he finds it impossible to do so. Even when the poison glass is placed to one side, it still ends up in his hand or in his wallet! This trick can be done over and over again. Besides the cards, you get an instruction booklet of 28 pages that also includes two dozen additional routines, and a set of envelopes and a plastic wallet also used in some versions.

$5

Glenn Comar
353 E. Sixth Ave.
Roselle, N.J. 07203

HOLY JOE

A card is shown or someone selects one. You hold this in one hand and ask a lady to reach into your trouser pocket to remove the hole that you have there. Usually she will decline so that you have to reach in yourself. You take out the invisible hole and throw it toward the card. Oh

yes, it lands all right, and there is a ¾-inch hole right through the very center of the card. No skill required.

$1

Glenn Comar
353 E. Sixth Ave.
Roselle, N.J. 07203

CARD CRASH-THROUGH

You lay a playing card and any small piece of paper on top of a transparent plastic pane about 5¼ inches square with rounded corners. Another piece of plastic goes on top, and four rubber bands are stretched around it all. Any spectator now taps into the middle of the top pane with a pencil, and immediately the card breaks through the lower pane. The little piece of paper, however, stays trapped inside where it belongs.

This is a marvelous little miracle. Any card can be used, the paper can have someone's initials written on it, and everything can be examined before and after. It doesn't seem possible.

$5

Glenn Comar
353 E. Sixth Ave.
Roselle, N.J. 07203

SIX-CARD REPEAT

This is a very funny item that can be used for children or adults. You begin telling a story about seeing a magician who had six cards (you count out six cards) and who threw away three of them (you remove three) and still had six left (you count out six cards again). In case anyone doesn't understand, you repeat the story. See, he had six cards (you count them out) and he threw away three (you do so) and had six left (you have six left). You keep on explaining what you saw the magician do, and it gets funnier and funnier until finally you end with, "I wonder how he did it." This is good sleight-of-hand and high-class comedy.

$4

Healey's Magic Co.
1612 Dickson Ave.
Scranton, Pa. 18509

TV CARD FRAME

This is a magical classic. A card is selected and torn into small pieces. The pieces are placed in an envelope and burned—except for one single piece, which is given to a spectator to hold. The magician takes the ashes and throws them at a flat plastic square held up in the air on two little pillars. Immediately the selected card appears between the two sheets of plastic. All that is missing is the piece the spectator is holding. The card is removed from the frame and the piece held by the spectator is seen to be the missing corner. It fits perfectly.

$29.50

Healey's Magic Co.
1612 Dickson Ave.
Scranton, Pa. 18509

FUTURE FORETOLD

Doug Henning performed this on *The Tonight Show* a couple of years ago, and it's terrific! You write a prediction and put it in an envelope. Then the spectator takes a deck of cards and begins dealing them out face up. The spectator can stop at any time. When that happens, the prediction is immediately seen to match—you have guessed in advance the card that would be face up on top of the stack! Or so it seems. The spectator has a free choice of where to stop, and no sleight-of-hand is required.

$5

Healey's Magic Co.
1612 Dickson Ave.
Scranton, Pa. 18509

DOT'S IMPOSSIBLE

Six cards are placed face down on the table. A person points to any card—and he has a completely free choice. The other cards are then shown, and each one has a large black spot on its face. The spectator turns his card over and it has a large red spot on its face. You can repeat this immediately.

$1.50

Al's Magic Shop
1205 Pennsylvania Ave. N.W.
Washington, D.C. 20004

EX-IT

A great prediction trick. A spectator places an X on a card while he holds the deck behind his back. He has no idea which card he marks. Yet you have correctly predicted which one it will be. Very easy to learn and perform. Any deck can be used.

$2

Al's Magic Shop
1205 Pennsylvania Ave. N.W.
Washington, D.C. 20004

THE HAUNTED HOUSE

Have you ever seen a ghost vanish? Five cards spell out the word HOUSE. They are picked up, redealt, but now spell the word GHOST. Then they are dealt out a third time, but they are blank! The GHOST has vanished. So easy to do a child can perform it.

$3

Al's Magic Shop
1205 Pennsylvania Ave. N.W.
Washington, D.C. 20004

HOLE IN ONE

Seven cards are shown front and back, one at a time. Someone selects a card and fires an imaginary bullet at the pack of seven cards, using his finger as a gun. Imagine everyone's surprise when the chosen card is removed with a ¼-inch hole drilled neatly through its center.

$2

Al's Magic Shop
1205 Pennsylvania Ave. N.W.
Washington, D.C. 20004

BLANK AND BLUE

You start out with a deck that's got red backs, and pull out the only card that has a blue back. You look at it, then bury it in the pack by cutting several times. Now your victim selects any card at random, looking at the faces only. By golly, if it isn't the only one with the blue back! He puts it back in the deck and you spread the cards to show that now they *all* have blue backs. Then you turn the deck face up and spread the cards again. This time they are all blank! All except for the spectator's chosen card, that is.

$4

Lou Tannen
1540 Broadway
New York, N.Y. 10036

OVERDOSE

You show two cards that are blank except for blue question marks printed on their faces. You ask your audience to select two cards from a deck, then place the two blank cards face to face. When you separate them, they still have the blue question marks on them, but they are also imprinted with the values of the selected cards. This one is real magic.

$3.50

Lou Tannen
1540 Broadway
New York, N.Y. 10036

THE SUBMERGED CARD MYSTERY

A glass is filled with water and an ordinary dish is placed over the glass. Now both are inverted, leaving the glass full of water. At this point, nothing can get into or out of the glass without spilling water all over the place. Now the inverted glass is covered with a handkerchief and placed aside, in full view of the audience.

A deck of cards is introduced, shuffled, and cut several times. A spectator is asked to peek at a card and remember it. The deck is never out of sight of the audience. Without any sleight-of-hand, the magician runs through the deck. There are now only fifty-one cards! One card is missing. The handkerchief is removed from the inverted glass of water and there, submerged in the water, is the card that was selected but a few moments earlier.

Unbelievable! Yes indeed. The glass of water is turned upright and the card is removed, dripping wet. There is no doubt that the card somehow got into the glass of water. There is no obvious explanation, and everything can be examined completely. No sleight-of-hand is required; the mystery is entirely self-working and can be performed only five minutes after you review the procedure.

$9.50

Lou Tannen
1540 Broadway
New York, N.Y. 10036

RISING ROPE OUT OF POCKET

The magician gets results with this one even after he seems to have failed twice.

First he shows a piece of rope about a foot long. He says he will hypnotize it and make it stand erect. No such luck. He gives up at last and puts the rope in his jacket pocket, saying, "That didn't work. Guess we'll do a card trick."

He has someone pick a card and shuffle it back into the pack. Two or three guesses about which one is the right card are all wrong. He puts the deck of cards in his jacket pocket and begins to explain, "This isn't my day," and goes on to explain why the rope trick failed, why the card trick failed, why . . . and meanwhile, slowly, seemingly without his knowing anything about it, the rope slowly rises out of his pocket rigidly, and the selected card is attached to the rope.

The magician pretends not to notice and keeps on talking as the rope continues to rise a full 12 inches into the air. The audience goes crazy and howls with delight.

$18.50

Lou Tannen
1540 Broadway
New York, N.Y. 10036

BERLAND'S BILL-IN-LEMON TRICK

Imagine this: You request someone in the audience to lend you a piece of currency of any denomination. The bill is marked by several spectators to prove that no duplicates are used. Then it is folded and placed in a handkerchief and given to someone from the audience to hold securely. A bag of lemons that has been on the table in full view all this time is then shown, and one lemon is chosen by a spectator. This lemon—there is no switch to another lemon—is placed in a napkin and is held by another spectator.

Now the impossible happens! The piece of currency vanishes from the handkerchief. Your hands are empty. The lemon is removed from the napkin. It is cut open and a bill is seen right in the center. The person who lent the money removes it and identifies it as the same one that was initialed by several people at the start of the trick. There are no assistants, no trick knives. This is the most subtle and direct method ever conceived, and has been performed at Hollywood's famous Magic Castle.

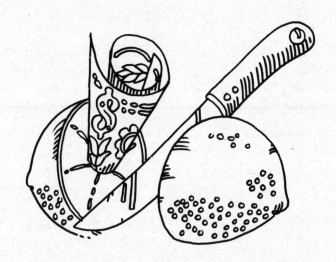

$10

Healey's Magic Co.
1612 Dickson Ave.
Scranton, Pa. 18509

MATHEMATICAL JOKER

There are five packs of cards, and from each one the spectator chooses one card freely. These five cards are placed on a stand so that only their backs can be seen by the audience.

Now the magician takes a full deck of cards out and has a second spectator choose one card, which he puts face down on the table. He announces a prediction—the total value of the cards on the stand will add up to the value of the card that is face down.

Everyone starts figuring and soon discovers that each of the cards on the stand has to be a two, because the highest value the face-down card can possibly have is ten.

The magician confesses that they have him trapped. He shows the cards in the deck that was just used—they are all tens. Pretty tricky! And he shows the cards in the other five decks. They are all twos. Everyone groans at this terrible example of cheating. Unfair! Unfair!

But wait! The face-down card is turned over. It's not a ten! It's a joker! The second spectator has chosen the only card in the deck that was not a ten! Has the magician failed? Don't be silly! When the five cards are reversed—remember, each was freely chosen—they spell out J-O-K-E-R!

This does not require sleight-of-hand, and all the cards and stands are provided. Just read the easy instructions and you can perform this incredible feat within minutes.

$6.50

Lou Tannen
1540 Broadway
New York, N.Y. 10036

SANDWICH SURPRISE

This is a funny, new, easy-to-do card trick with amusing props and a novel effect. A deck of cards is fanned face up and then turned face down. A card is selected and removed from the deck. It is examined and replaced anywhere in the deck, which is shuffled.

The magician lays three cards from the deck face down in front of the spectator and says that

whichever card the spectator picks will be his chosen card. If not, the magician will buy his lunch. Oops! The card is the wrong one. In fact, none of the cards is the one that was chosen, and the magician admits he has been stuck.

He then produces a lunch bag and pulls out a sandwich wrapped in wax paper. After much humorous byplay between him and the surprised spectator, the card is finally found inside the sandwich.

Everything is furnished—the cards, the lunch bag, even the sandwich.

$4

H. L. Moorehouse
1008 Pearl St.
Ypsilanti, Mich. 48197

FAKE GAMBLING ACT

Do you want to apparently expose card sharks? Want to show a lot of skill with a deck of cards, even if you don't have any skill to show? Step right up, help is on the way! You can put on an interesting and entertaining demonstration of how gamblers cheat and make your friends think that you have become a real wizard. The methods described in this manuscript require no skills at all, though you apparently deal the second card from the top, the bottom card, incredible poker hands, whatever you want. You can even be blindfolded and deal poker in a winning way.

$2

Guaranteed Magic
27 Bright Rd.
Hatboro, Pa. 19040

CARD IN BALLOON

A freely selected card is taken from an unprepared deck, initialed, and returned. The deck is sealed in an ordinary card case. Then a balloon is inflated and set in a holder. The cards in the case are placed on the base of the stand. The balloon goes bang and the initialed card is found.

The apparatus is made of metal and is chrome-plated. No worries—it is all self-contained.

$22

Abbott's Magic Co.
Colon, Mich. 49040

SUPERIOR CARD SWORD

The magician fans a deck of cards and shows that each one is different. Then three members of the audience each choose a card and return it to the deck, which is thoroughly shuffled. Now the magician brings out a sword and asks a spectator to toss the cards into the air. As the cards come down, the magician stabs at them with the sword and—lo and behold!—all three chosen cards are found impaled on the sword tip and blade. This is an exciting classical effect that will liven up any card act with extra drama.

$40

Chu's Magic Studio
401 Chatham Rd.
T.S.T.
P.O. Box 5221
Kowloon, Hong Kong

DELUXE CARD STAR

A spectacular revelation of a chosen card—in fact, five chosen cards. A pack is shuffled and five spectators each choose a card. These are inserted back into the deck and it is shuffled.

Out comes a five-pointed star with long points on it, all made of shiny brass, and the deck is thrown against it. The selected cards mysteriously all appear on the five points of the metal star.

This is visible magic at its best!

$80

Chu's Magic Studio
401 Chatham Rd.
T.S.T.
P.O. Box 5221
Kowloon, Hong Kong

NU-POWER RISING CARDS

Someone once said that if you have a hundred ways of finding a chosen card and only one way of revealing it, the effect is that you know only one card trick. But if you know a hundred ways of revealing the chosen card and one way of finding it, the effect is that you know a hundred card tricks.

This is a fantastic method of revealing the chosen card. It is eerie and delightful. Watch what happens:

A member of the audience shuffles a deck of cards and then chooses any one freely. It may be initialed. It is placed back in the deck and the pack is placed in an interesting holder that allows the front of the bottom card to be seen clearly. It is a kind of skeleton frame for a deck of cards. Whenever you are ready, the chosen card rises slowly from the deck and stays aloft. More cards will rise later on if you wish.

This is foolproof and self-contained. It requires no strings, springs, weights, faked decks, compulsory card choices, adding things to the cards, taking things away from the cards, etc.

$42

Abbott's Magic Co.
Colon, Mich, 49040

FACE-DOWN POKER

This is a new card trick that will cause your friends to sit up and take notice.

You show four cards front and back. They are put face down and magically turn face up. For a climax, they turn into four aces. Then you show the cards front and back again.

This comes complete with a carrying case and instructions.

$3

John Cornelius
430 Elmwood
San Antonio, Tex. 78212

FULL-COLOR INSURANCE POLICY

A card is selected and returned to the deck. The magician runs through the pack and pulls out what he says is the selected card. Wrong! He tries again . . . and again. Pretty soon he is beginning to get panicky, so he reaches for his insurance policy and begins to read the fine print about the purpose and conditions and so on, all of which are comedy lines written on the policy.

Finally he opens it up to full size and shows a huge, colorful picture (18×22 inches) of the chosen card!

$2.50

Guaranteed Magic
27 Bright Rd.
Hatboro, Pa. 19040

UNIQUE CARD RISE CHEST

Any number of cards are selected, marked for identification later, and then replaced in the deck. The deck is tossed into a neat, attractive chest. At the performer's command the cover of the chest rises very slowly as a card rises out of it. The card is removed and the cover slams shut. This may be repeated as often as you like, and all of the cards that appear are the original ones. No duplicates are used.

There are no threads to worry about, no special manipulation required to rearrange the cards, etc. Further, you can do this up close and with any deck of cards. Truly a high-quality item that you will use many times and find many different applications for.

$22

Aladdin Magic Shop
110 S. High St.
Columbus, Ohio 43215

THE DIRTY DEAL

An amusing close-up trick with a knockout finish. Five cards are shown back and front. The backs are blue. One card is placed face down on the table. A red-backed card is removed from a wallet (supplied) and placed on top of the cards in the hand—all cards now have red backs! One is placed face down on the table.

A card with a different blue back is taken from the wallet, placed on top of the cards—bingo—

all cards now have the same color and back. One is removed and placed alongside the two tabled cards.

An odd card with a multi-colored back is then introduced from the wallet to the packet of cards—bam—all cards now have multi-colored backs. One is placed on the table.

The unbelievable then takes place. Turning over the cards that remain in his hand, the performer throws them across the table—and each of the nine cards employed in the trick has a completely different back design and color!

A complete outfit, including illustrated instruction brochure, the wallet from which the trick is presented, and a complete set of cards.

$4

Bruce Cervon
443 N. Gardner Ave.
Los Angeles, Cal. 90036

CARD CASTLES

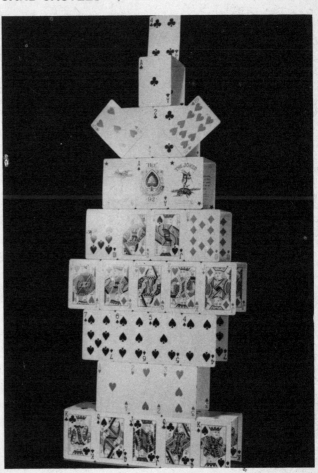

Is all of life really a house of cards? Well, now you can have the card castle that impresses everyone.

$3.50

Mystofire Magic
5301-C Bissonet
Bellaire, Tex. 77401

DIZZY DIAMONDS

A great little card trick that is completely mechanical. A card is selected and replaced into the pack. The performer says that he will reveal the selected card in a most mysterious way. The deck is set aside and a small felt case is shown. The performer removes a beautiful diamond-studded Lucite plaque and asks the following questions: Was your card the six of diamonds, the four, the three, the ace? None of these. The plaque is replaced in the felt holder. The spectator is asked if he selected his card from the deck. He did. The plaque is again removed and shown to the spectator: Was his card the three of diamonds? *No.* The performer then rubs the plaque on his shirt sleeve and turns it over, and sure enough there is a large seven all laid out in diamonds on the plaque. A great card trick to carry with you. Complete with routine and plaques. Use your own cards.

$5

Jack Miller Enterprises
119 Weymouth Rd.
Syracuse, N.Y. 13205

KUSS KASTLE KLIMAX

The magician, for his last effect, introduces a black cloth bag, which he unfolds, and removes from it a pack of Mini-Cards. These are shuffled and a spectator is requested to remove one, remember it, and return it to the pack. The pack is then fanned and dropped into the bag. The magician explains that he can mentally perceive the name of the chosen card and produce it from the bag simply by utilizing his extraordinary sense of touch. He then holds the bag up high, so he cannot see in, reaches in, and pulls out a card with its back to the audience. This is turned around and . . . it is the wrong card. This is returned to the bag "to make it doubly hard," and another card is removed. This is also found to be the wrong card. "Isn't this a great finale?" asks the magician. He then requests the name of the chosen card and states that he will certainly get it this time. Then he reaches in and pulls from the bag a card castle 20 inches high and 8 inches wide with the chosen card at the peak! And, as a climax, "The End" is boldly printed on the castle, making a fine closing for any close-up act.

$15

Jack Miller Enterprises
119 Weymouth Rd.
Syracuse, N.Y. 13205

SEEING IS BELIEVING

A bill ($1 or $5) is borrowed and the serial number is noted. The bill is then folded twice and *slowly and deliberately torn in half*. The halves are displayed, put together and *torn again!* The pieces are put into a paper clip and handed back to the lender. When he removes it, it is found fully restored, and it has the same serial number. *You* will have a ball watching their reaction when they see the bill ripped in half.

$3.25

Cards by Martin
507 W. Avenue H-8
Lancaster, Cal. 93534

MIRACLE MATES

The pieces of four cards which have been cut in half are openly mixed, yet they magically pair up! Can be repeated immediately and is always ready for presentation. Spectators are shown the fronts and backs of all eight half-cards, and the cards are handled slowly and deliberately.

It's easy to do but hard to believe.

$3

Micky Hades International
Box 2242
Seattle, Wash. 98111

ZIG-ZAG CARD

The magician has a jumbo card examined and signed. He places the card in a finely tooled chrome-trimmed Plexiglas cabinet just large enough to accommodate the card. Three doors open to show the signed card inside. The performer proceeds to sever the card in thirds with two playing cards. The doors are now closed and the center section is pushed to the performer's extreme right. The magician opens the doors and the signed card is plainly visible to all. The procedure is now reversed, and the signed card is given away as a souvenir of this memorable event.

$125

Danny Korem
417 Tiffany Trail
Richardson, Tex. 75081

BACK TO BLUE

Aw, c'mon now! This *can't* work the way it's supposed to, but by golly, it sure does! You start out with a deck that's got red backs, and pull out the only card that has a blue back. You look at it, then bury it in the pack by cutting several times. In fact, you'll cut it as often as your audience likes. Now your "victim" selects any card at random, looking at the faces only. It turns out that the card he selected is the one with the blue back! As an added kicker, he puts it back in the deck, and you ribbon-spread the cards to show that now they *all* have blue backs! When we first saw this one demonstrated, one of the magicians commented that it was good, but it needed a more climactic finish. The demonstrator looked at him for a minute, then turned the deck face up and ribbon-spread them once again. The cards were all blank! All blank, that is, except for the card the spectator selected, which is still printed.

$4

The Jokers Wild
Box 513
Cape Coral, Fla. 33904

DOUBLE TAKE

Four cards are fanned, face down, and one is freely chosen. It is displayed, then mixed with the others. The spectator is asked to keep a poker face while the faces of the cards are shown, one at a time, so that the performer cannot tell which is the selected card. Actually, three of the cards are the same as the chosen card, and the spectator will soon let you know. You act puzzled, spread the cards face up. All are different; the chosen card has vanished. You produce it from your pocket or wallet. It comes all ready to work. No sleights.

$3

Lee's Studio of Magic
319 N. High St.
Millville, N.J. 08332

SHELL-GAME CARD TRICK

This is the three-shell game with cards. You show how you were "taken" with the three-shell game. Display three cards with nutshells on the back. Two cards are blank-faced and the third shows a "pea." Cards are mixed and shown, but the pea has vanished! All three "shells" are empty! But, when shown again the pea appears under *each* shell! Finally you explain whichever shell is picked you always wind up "behind the 8-ball" and a large 8-ball appears under each shell!

Mechanical, easy-to-do. Comes complete with special cards printed in three colors, illustrated directions, and patter.

$2.50

Nick Trost Magic
1382 Virginia Ave.
Columbus, Ohio 43212

HALF-WILD DECK

A new deck that drives 'em wild. You show a deck cut in two parts. Someone selects a card from each half-pack, and when placed together the selected halves match—back and front! You then show a "prediction" card and it matches selected half-cards! But that's not all—one half-pack is spread and it has no backs—the other half no faces! A double-whammy climax! Easy to do—no rough and smooth. Complete with special bridge-size deck and routined directions.

$5.50

Nick Trost Magic
1382 Virginia Ave.
Columbus, Ohio 43212

ACE IN THE HOLE

A worthless poker hand changes to four aces. Show five cards dealt in stud-poker fashion (one down, four up). You don't even have a pair. The down card is no help and is laid aside. When the other cards are shown again—they've changed to three aces. The hole card is turned up and it has changed to the fourth ace!

$2.50

Nick Trost Magic
1382 Virginia Ave.
Columbus, Ohio 43212

TOMMY WINDSOR'S PET INSURANCE POLICY

You talk about how pets now have everything including hospitals, doctors, psychiatrists, cemeteries, etc. So now you have taken out pet insurance to guarantee that your "Animal Rummy" miracle works. You show the policy. And this is just where the fun begins. You have a spectator choose a card from an "Animal Rummy Deck" and you attempt to tell him the animal he chose, repeatedly failing to do so. Finally, you open up your policy to see how to file a claim and the policy unfolds to a giant 17×22-inch picture of the animal the spectator chose. The policy pays off, all right, with applause and laughter that'll bring down the house. For the largest or smallest audience, for kids or adults.

Can be carried in a pocket but with a big climax. Complete with insurance policy and complete instructions.

$2

Jacobs Productions
Box 362
Pomeroy, Ohio 45769

CARD VANISH

A real show stopper, it has a large stage size and measures 20×8×1 inches thick, which makes it very deceptive. Show the giant frame. Place a giant card into one of the two compartments and tell everyone that you will make the card vanish. Everyone will yell that they saw the card slide to the other side. As you make it vanish from the second compartment, they again see the card slide. At the end, you open both doors, and the card has vanished!

$25

Jose's Studio
17-C Wallace St.
Belleville, N.J. 07109

POKER MYSTERY

Almost a miracle! The magician shows five cards, backs and fronts; one is an ace and the four others are fives. Mysteriously, the ace changes into a five and the fives all change into aces! Easy to learn!

$2

International Magic
7370 N.W. 72nd Ave.
Miami, Fla. 33166

CARD SWORD CANE

The magician has three cards selected by members of the audience. They return their cards to the deck. Each spectator remembers his card. The magician displays a cane, tosses the deck into the air, and makes a stab with the cane into the cards as they flutter down. The cane impales three cards. "The first gentleman," says the magician. "What was your card?" "Seven of spades." "The seven of spades," says the magician, ripping that card off the cane and displaying the card. Likewise, the second card is correct. It, too, is ripped off the cane and shown or tossed to the audience. The third card, at the tip of the cane, turns out to be the *wrong card*. The magician tears it off the cane and tosses it aside. "Well," says the magician, "What was your card?" "The king of diamonds," the spectator answers. Suddenly the magician's cane changes into a large silk with the king of diamonds printed upon it!

Complete set includes specially gimmicked Fantasio's Vanishing Cane, several hole-punched cards, and 24×36-inch silk with the jumbo king of diamonds printed on it in full colors.

$30

International Magic
7370 N.W. 72nd Ave.
Miami, Fla. 33166

MAGIC CARDS

The magician has two spectators each think of a card. He proceeds to write his impression of each on a blank-faced card with a marker. The cards are placed in a rack in full view of audience. The magician now produces an ordinary deck of cards and asks spectators to announce their thought-of cards. These are removed from the deck and placed in the rack. When the rack is turned, the magician's impressions are seen to match the selected cards.

Card rack is made of gleaming black and clear Lucite and revolves.

$14.50

Healey's Magic Co.
1612 Dickson Ave.
Scranton, Pa. 18509

CARD MINT

Watch cards turn into money . . . right before your audience's eyes. Remove two cards from the deck, rub them face to face, and a full-blown dollar bill appears between them. You then rub them back to back, and another bill appears. The cards are shown back and front and are discarded. You can then do a money trick.

$3.50

Cards by Martin
507 W. Avenue H-8
Lancaster, Cal. 93534

DOUBLE-DOOR CARD VANISH

This trick is a real professional! Claim that you will make a giant card vanish. Open one of the compartments and place the card inside. Pretend to make the card vanish—but your audience will see it slide across to the other side. Go through a sucker act with your audience and finally slide the card back.

The finale: open both doors and the card has vanished! Self-working and easy to assemble. Measures 18×18×1 inches.

$15

Zanadu
165 Hancock Ave.
Jersey City, N.J. 07307

CARD-IN-ORANGE TRICK

This trick will establish you as a real magician! You show a deck and prove the cards are all different. A card is then selected by a spectator, and he is told to tear the card into pieces, but to retain one piece for identification. The balance of the pieces are burned, after being inserted in an envelope. An orange is then cut open by the spectator and in the center is found the selected card, with a piece missing from one corner. The piece held by the spectator fits perfectly! No sleight-of-hand required. Just the clearly printed instructions and the deck of special "forcing" cards which is furnished. You can do this astonishing trick within five minutes after reading instructions.

$2

Magic and Fun
P.O. Box 1936
Grand Central Station
New York, N.Y. 10017

COMPUTER CARDS

In the age of computers, you need at least one card trick with computers.

The magician shows a number of normal computer cards and allows the spectator to select one. It is placed into the computer and a deck of cards is introduced. The deck is shown to be normal, and the computer card is removed to help select a playing card.

They are both placed back into the computer one at a time. A moment later, when they are removed, the computer card has the name and suit of the selected card printed along the top and the respective holes punched out below.

Everything can be examined, there is nothing to get rid of at the end, and the illusion can be repeated using a different card. Comes complete with computer cards and computer. Use your own deck of playing cards.

$5

Ramsey Magic & Novelty Co.
72 E. Main St.
Ramsey, N.J. 07446

THE KISS TRICK

This is a honey of a trick that will get you all sorts of attention. Imagine finding a selected card with the help of a beautiful girl and her kiss! You will love it—and so will she.

The amazing climax of this trick is that the magician gets a free kiss. Clever, yet easy for anyone with a little card experience (or anyone willing to get experience).

$1.50

Universal Productions
1315 Laurel Ln.
Martinsville, Va. 24112

SUPER BALLOON TRICK

An attractive stand is on the magician's table, along with a small balloon. The balloon is blown up and put on the stand. Three cards are selected by audience members, and torn to small pieces. The magician collects the pieces, and one of the spectators keeps a piece from one of the cards. The magician now throws the pieces to the balloon, which bursts with a loud bang.

The cards that were chosen are all seen to be lined up on the chrome stand. One of the cards has a missing piece, and the one held by the spectator matches the hole perfectly.

This is fully automatic.

$50

Tom Fitzgerald
2814 Washington St.
Wilmington, Del. 19802

DEVANO RISING CARDS

Any number of cards, as many as ten if you like, are freely selected and returned to the deck. The spectators can shuffle and cut, and yet at your command the chosen cards mysteriously begin to rise into the air.

The cards can be initialed or marked for identification—they are the same cards. They will rise slowly or fast, just as you wish. You can even put the deck in a glass tumbler and the cards will rise.

Here is a sensational method of revealing a chosen card.

$15

Jose's Studio
17-C Wallace St.
Belleville, N.J. 01709

4 | COINS AND CURRENCY

Since medieval times when alchemists labored to change base metals into gold, money has had a place in magic. Why not? It is the coin of the realm that can buy us the material things we want, and if it doesn't buy happiness, few of us would deny that it makes life easier.

Wouldn't it be wonderful if all we had to do was to make a wish or wave a wand to be rich? That's why few tricks please an audience more than those in which a magician plucks coins from the air or produces a shining stream of silver to flood the stage. This is sleight-of-hand at its most sophisticated. It is not only magical, it can be beautiful.

Performing magic with money can be divided into a number of categories. There is the production of coins from the air; there is the vanishing and reappearance of coins or bills; there are coins that produce special effects. Magic dealers offer highly developed special equipment for doing many of these fine tricks, but to make any of them look effortless and exciting takes skillful manipulation that can only result from hours and hours of practice.

But, for most of us, working with money is its own reward. Consider the coin. We handle a variety of them every day. We use them to pay our way on public transportation, to buy a newspaper, to make change. Now, think of the fancy manipulation that can be done with these small pieces of metal. They can be twirled about the fingers and hidden in the palm of the hand to disappear and reappear, to shrink and grow and change form. It is the fact that coins are so common to our everyday life that makes them so fascinating when they are the tools of magic.

This familiarity makes us less suspicious when a magician produces surprises—turning dimes into pennies or vice-versa; always flipping heads, or tails, as called; making coins multiply—that are simple with the special apparatus and effects available. Little wonder, that the "miser's dream" trick, in which a steady stream of coins is collected from the air, is one of the most famous of all time.

Or look at currency. It is easily recognizable, identified by serial number, and has value. In our daily lives it disappears with use but the wonder of making it vanish and then reappear; of doubling a bill's face value, or seeing a bill multiply is a wizardry audiences never tire of watching.

Magic with money may be the most intriguing of all sleight-of-hand. But the payoff is not just in the proper equipment, it's in the practice to perfect manipulation. To date, no magic in the world has eliminated the need for most of us to work to produce money, even when it's an illusion.

WASHOUT

Surprisingly easy to do, yet impossible to figure out. A brass washer and a Kennedy half-dollar are shown. The washer is placed on top of the half-dollar, the coin being visible through the washer's hole. The audience is told not to blink or they will miss the miracle . . . and washout . . . instantly, the half-dollar visibly changes into an American penny! The half-dollar has vanished completely! The washer may now be examined. This coin effect has been created through the art of precision machining. Three routines are included.

$4

Jose's Studio
17-C Wallace St.
Belleville, N.J. 07109

BLINK

A penny is placed between the folds of a coin folder, where it can be seen through the transparent cellophane window. The coin folder is shown absolutely empty and can even be examined. There are no threads, no wires, no mirrors.

$2

James Rainho Products
14 Windsor Rd.
Medford, Mass. 02155

THE TOPPER

This is a special bottle top or cork that matches a well-known brand so that it can be easily substituted. A half-dollar is made to vanish and then made to reappear inside a glass bottle. No skill is necessary, but the magician needs his own folding coin.

$6.50

Exhibitor Sales Presentations
P.O. Box 203
Merrimac, Mass. 01860

STACK OF QUARTERS

Six quarters are borrowed and placed on the back of your hand. A dollar bill is rolled into a cone and placed over the coins. At the magic word, the coins pass through the hand, and when the cone is removed it appears the quarters have changed into dimes. Gimmick coins look natural. A little practice will make this a big hit.

$12.50

The Emporium of Magic
Building A, Suite 110
17220 W. Eight Mile Rd.
Southfield, Mich. 48075

BILL TUBE/SALT SHAKER

The magician borrows a piece of currency from a person in the audience. It is marked for identification and later rolled into a tube shape. An elastic band is snapped around it and it is then wrapped in a handkerchief, also borrowed from a member of the audience and given to the bill's lender to hold. He is also given a handsome salt shaker and asked to sprinkle some on the handkerchief. The magician snatches away the cloth and holds it aloft. The bill has vanished. It later reappears inside the salt shaker. Only one piece of currency is used.

$16

Glenn Comar
353 E. Sixth Ave.
Roselle, N.J. 07203

HALF BACK

A penny is inserted into a Boston (bulldog) paper clip and both sides are shown. As you drop the penny out of the clip, it changes into a 50-cent piece right before the eyes of the audience. Very clever and easy to do. A good quick trick on its own or with others to create a super magic money routine.

$8

Steve Dusheck Jr.
1000 Seybert St.
Hazleton, Pa. 18201

$3

Guaranteed Magic
27 Bright Rd.
Hatboro, Pa. 19040

WELL I NEVER!

A new coin disappearance trick destined to become a classic trick. It is all so simple and ordinary—people marvel at its impossibility.

Three matches are used to form a triangle, and a coin is placed in the center. An ordinary playing card is placed completely hiding everything, and on this the matchbox is laid. Slowly, carefully, the box and card are removed and the coin has completely vanished! Spectators can remove articles! They can make the triangle!

FOLDING COINS

The magician borrows a half-dollar and an empty bottle. With the spectator holding onto the bottle, the magician knocks the borrowed coin through the bottom of the bottle. After the bottle has been examined, the magician proceeds to shake the coin out through the neck of the bottle. The items are returned, and the audience is speechless.

$5

Flosso Hornmann
304 W. 34th St.
New York, N.Y. 10001

COIN CARD

This special device is something the serious magician will really enjoy using. Two completely different effects are possible with it.

1.—The classic coin assembly. Four half-dollars are placed under four playing cards. One at a time, each coin leaves its card until all four of them have gathered under one card. In this rou-

tine, sleight-of-hand has been replaced by subtle, easy-to-do moves made possible by the ingenious apparatus.

2.—A visual quickie. Show a half-dollar at your finger tips. It instantly changes into a playing card the same value as the one the spectator chose.

$10

Steve Dusheck Jr.
1000 Seybert Street
Hazleton, Pa. 18201

MYSTIFYING TRICK RAG

Borrow a dollar bill from a spectator and roll it into a tube. A red rag initialed by the spectator is placed inside and then plastic caps are put on both ends of the bill so that the tube is sealed. The spectator holds his dollar bill in full view of the audience.

A second dollar bill is borrowed from another spectator and is rolled and capped in the same way. The red rag transfers magically from the first tube into the second one, and is finally identified by the one who initialed it. No duplicate props are required.

$4

Healey's Magic Co.
1612 Dickson Ave.
Scranton, Pa. 18509

POP

A real coin is pushed through a solid piece of rubber by a spectator who has no idea how it's done! Absolutely the most startling thing you have ever seen. Easy to do if you know how. Impossible if you don't.

$2

Al's Magic Shop
1205 Pennsylvania Ave. N.W.
Washington, D.C. 20004

DUSHECK'S DOLLAR

A real dollar is shown on both sides, then folded in half. A knife is inserted into the fold to slit the dollar in half. The pieces are spread apart and shown on both sides. Each half is then held by the ends with the torn sections overlapping. Pulling the ends of the dollar instantly and visibly restores it.

This is easy, visible magic. You use the same dollar over and over. No refills to buy. It is self-contained—no extra devices to hide. Comes complete with instructions and sample play bill.

$3

Steve Dusheck Jr.
1000 Seybert St.
Hazleton, Pa. 18201

NICKELS TO DIMES

Place four nickels on anyone's hand and place a small cap over the coins. When the cap is lifted, the nickels have changed to dimes. The cap may be examined closely. No one who is not a magician will figure out what happened. This is an ideal pocket miracle.

$2

Flosso Hornmann
304 W. 34th St.
New York, N.Y. 10001

PRIDE

A borrowed half-dollar penetrates through a folded handkerchief into a tumbler. That's all—but it's beautiful to watch, and can be repeated at once. No fake coins are involved, just a little thingamabob that works without any skill on your part.

$5

Glenn Comar
353 E. Sixth Ave.
Roselle, N.J. 07203

DOLLAR PUNCH

This sounds impossible, but read on anyway. A real dollar bill is shown and the serial number is noted. The dollar is folded into eighths, placed into a real paper hole punch, and punched. The bill is removed, unfolded, and shown. The serial number is again shown to make sure it's the same bill.

The punched-out pieces are dropped on the dollar, which is folded and placed back into the punch. Now the magician gently shakes the pieces "back into the holes."

The dollar bill is unfolded and shown completely restored, and the serial number is shown once more to be the same. The trick is easy to do and can be repeated instantly. It comes with instructions, paper hole punch, sample play money, and additional routines and ideas. You supply your own real money.

$3

Steve Dusheck Jr.
1000 Seybert Street
Hazleton, Pa. 18201

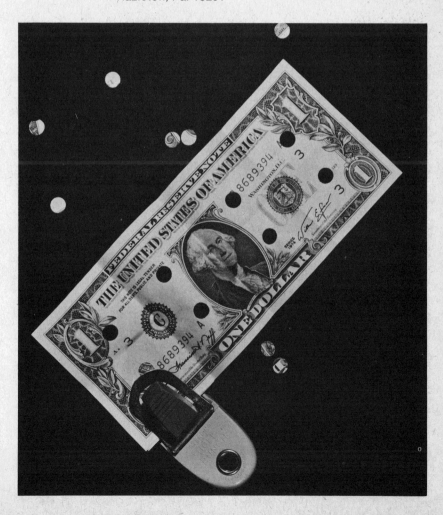

MIRACLE VANISHER

A borrowed ring or any marked coin up to a half-dollar vanishes from the magician's hand and appears inside his jacket pocket. No elastic, no clips to hold onto the ring and damage it.

$14.50

Exhibitor Sales Presentations
P.O. Box 203
Merrimac, Mass. 01860

THE VANISHING NICKEL

Did you ever wish you could be a brilliant coin performer without spending years learning complex sleights and elaborate finger manipulations? Now's your chance!

You can even wear short sleeves with this one if you want to, and use only one hand. Show both sides of the hand, and the coin vanishes and returns with no false moves. Has been done on television.

$10.50

John Cornelius
430 Elmwood
San Antonio, Tex. 78212

SUPER BILL TUBE

A bill tube is one of the standard items that goes with any magical act involving money handling both onstage and close-up. Here are some of the effects that are possible with this dandy brass item:

1.—Performer borrows a dollar bill and has it initialed by someone, who also writes down the serial number. The bill is wrapped in a handkerchief and held by a volunteer. The performer shows a small tube that has a bar running through it that is secured by means of a padlock. The handkerchief is whipped away, and the spectator's hands are shown empty. The spectator picks up the tube and unlocks it, and there is the borrowed bill, complete with the same initials and serial number. You can perform this five minutes after you receive the apparatus. It is entirely mechanical and completely mystifying.

2.—A small silk is poked into the empty tube. The lid is put on, the bolt put through it, and the padlock secured. It is covered with a handkerchief and given to a spectator to hold. Later, the spectator unlocks the tube and finds the silk has vanished.

Obviously there are many more things possible with this amazing and useful device. You are limited only by your imagination. Full instructions and many ideas are included with the tube, which is carefully crafted from brass. The tube may be inspected by the audience with no chance of discovering its secret.

$12.50

Lou Tannen
1540 Broadway
New York, N.Y. 10036

MONEY MAKER

Need a couple of bucks? Turn them out yourself with this new, all-plastic pocket-size money maker. Put a piece of white paper in one side of

the machine, run the knob, and out pops a fresh, crisp dollar bill (or $5 or $10 or $20 or $50—whatever your budget can afford!)

Put in another piece of paper and out pops another bill. It acts like a small printing press. Use it to change the color of a piece of ribbon or to have messages and the names of selected cards appear on a blank piece of paper. There are many other possibilities.

$2

Lou Tannen
1540 Broadway
New York, N.Y. 10036

MAGIC COIN BOX

Here is one of the easiest, yet most effective pocket tricks in magic. Borrow a coin from a spectator and have it marked or scratched for identification. Place it in your pocket and pull out a small box covered with rubber bands. This is handed to the spectator to open. When the rubber bands are removed, the box is opened to reveal another, smaller box, also covered with rubber bands. This box is opened and inside is a small bag, closed with a rubber band. The spectator opens the bag, and inside is his coin—not a

duplicate, but the exact coin that he marked just a few moments before. This is a tremendous effect, and very easy to do.

$1.50

The Wizard
1136 Pearl St.
Boulder, Colo. 80302

$1.35 TRICK

Four coins, a dime, a quarter, and two half-dollars are placed, one at a time, into the performer's fist. When the fist is opened, all the coins have mysteriously disappeared, leaving only a half-dollar. The half-dollar that remains can be freely passed for examination. Using this set of four coins, you can make three or four coins vanish, penetrate a table, or change places. It is precision-made from real solid coins. A bang ring and four original routines are included.

$17.50

Jose's Studio
17-C Wallace St.
Belleville, N.J. 07109

THE INVISIBLE COIN

The magician removes a deck of cards from its case and ribbon-spreads them on the table in front of him. He then sets a clear glass tumbler on the table. Showing his hands to be empty (and they are), he explains that he is about to perform a coin trick using the cards and the glass. He gathers up the cards and places the empty glass, mouth down, on top of the deck. He then displays an invisible penny and sets it on the top of the inverted tumbler. He states that he will slap the penny and it will penetrate the glass. As he does this a clink is heard as a coin appears under the glass on top of the deck of cards. But wait, it is a quarter, not a penny! He removes the glass and sets it on the table. Everyone can plainly see the quarter. Magician then lets the coin slide off the deck of cards into the glass, where to the surprise of all it is now a

penny! Cards are again spread out across the table. Take our word for it that no skill is involved. No sleights. The fellow with all thumbs can do this one and fool the wise ones. Complete with cards and glass.

$5

Guaranteed Magic
27 Bright Rd.
Hatboro, Pa. 19040

COIN MAGIC

The great classic of coin magic. Four coins are placed into a small, round metal cylinder, completely filling it. A cap is placed on. The cylinder is then placed on the back of the hand. Mysteriously, the coins penetrate the hand and box and fall on top of table. The box is then opened and found empty. It is then passed out for examination. May also be used for penetrating a table or cards.

$4.50

Healey's Magic Co.
1612 Dickson Ave.
Scranton Pa. 18509

BY THE HANDFUL

For years a favorite trick of magicians has been to change a penny into a dime. Now it's better than ever, because after doing just that, you change a whole handful of pennies into dimes.

This mystery is easy to do, yet it is so baffling that it's used by many professional magicians. You will enjoy doing it and your audience will enjoy watching it.

Two well-made gimmicks and instructions. There have been many imitators, but this version is the best.

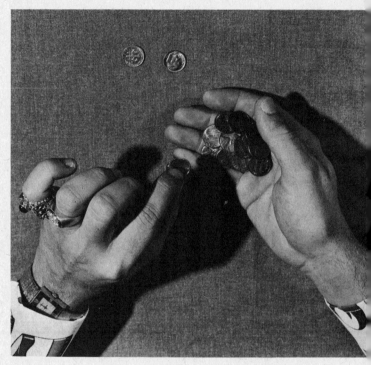

$4

Steve Dusheck Jr.
1000 Seybert St.
Hazleton, Pa. 18201

DELBEN QUARTER PENETRATION

Two coins are carried in a small plastic box. They are removed and the box is recapped. The coins are placed on top of the cap and covered with a card. One coin penetrates into the box instantly!

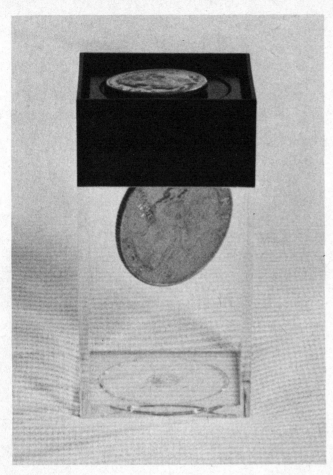

$3.75

Delben Co.
P.O. Box 3535
Springfield, Mo. 65804

HEADLINER (HEADOUT)

Here's a nice pocket trick you'll always carry with you. Passing your hand over a half-dollar changes it into an English penny. Another magical pass and it's a 50-cent piece again. Upon repeating these passes, some of the spectators will think the coin is a "fake" with a penny on one side and half-dollar on the other.

Imagine their surprise when the half-dollar reappears with the head cut out and missing. This coin is immediately handed out for examination. The head piece is then removed from your pocket and also is handed out. It fits into the half-dollar. The coins are machined and hand-crafted to make the effect easy to do.

$10

Steve Dusheck Jr.
1000 Seybert St.
Hazleton, Pa. 18201

KELLAR COIN CATCHER

Another way to do the miser's dream for those who have a little more ability to manipulate coins. No special glass or bucket is required. With this catcher, you can drop the coins into a borrowed champagne glass or (if you feel rich) toss them to the audience for an effect they will never forget.

This device is made to contain about sixteen U.S. half-dollars and to produce them one at a time at the tips of the fingers. It can be used in a wide array of effects and the creative magician will quickly think of many other uses for it.

$7.50

Lou Tannen
1540 Broadway
New York, N.Y. 10036

VISIBLE MISER'S DREAM

All of the money in the world seems to be yours with this wonderful effect. The magician reaches into thin air and plucks forth a coin, and then another, and another, as long as he cares to keep it up.

Traditionally, this trick called for long hours of practice to master the subtle and intricate coin moves. Now a simple mechanical device makes the trick easy. Your hands seem to be empty at all times. And yet a grab at the air and one, or even three or four coins are caught at the finger tips and actually tossed into the large, clear glass tumbler provided. The secret lies in the tumbler, which is made of handsome heavy-duty glass and is cleverly constructed to conceal a number of coins and release them when and as wanted.

Five or ten coins are used and reused over and over until you seem to produce fifty or a hundred coins! This is a self-contained trick; no sleight-of-hand is required.

$6

Lou Tannen
1540 Broadway
New York, N. Y. 10036

WONDERFUL COIN PAIL

Here is another means of making the miser's dream into a reality. As usual, you snatch a large number of coins from the air, one at a time, and keep it up for a long time. Merely reach into the air and "catch" them. Once you have the coin, toss it into the pail.

The mechanism for delivering the coins is built right in. A beautiful item.

$125

Lou Tannen
1540 Broadway
New York, N.Y. 10036

THE OKITO BOX

It is a small solid brass box made to hold four half-dollars or silver dollars. While many effects are possible, the basic routine is this: The magician can borrow a coin, place it in the box, and instantly cause it to penetrate through the box, and his hand! This can be repeated, and the box can be thoroughly examined. Also available are additional boxes for more effects. Information on these is available upon request. Basic instructions are included, but for more detailed routines you may want to purchase the *Okito*

Coin Box Routines of Mohammed Bey, $3.50. While the Okito box is not self-working, its use is easy to learn if you're willing to spend half an hour with it. It is handmade from solid brass. It's a beautiful piece of magic.

Half-dollar or silver-dollar size $15.00

The Wizard
1136 Pearl St.
Boulder, Colo. 80302

OKITO COIN BOX

This is a highly polished round box made of solid brass and perfectly weighted. Coins appear in it, disappear from it, and penetrate through the box. Dozens of famous effects are possible, and a complete routine is included with the instructions. This is a simple, elegant item.

$8

Flosso Hornmann
304 W. 34th St.
New York, N.Y. 10001

FANTASTIC NO-NAME OKITO COIN BOX

The coin box invented by Okito (Theo Bamberg) has many uses in magic. This improved version has an unusual climax.

A half-dollar is placed into the precision-made brass box and covered with a lid. This is then placed on the back of the hand, and the half-dollar penetrates right through the box and the hand. Next, five half-dollars are used, and they also penetrate through the hand.

However, when the spectator attempts to replace the coins into the box, he fails. The box has vanished and in its place is a solid brass cylinder engraved with a comic inscription.

$12

H. L. Moorehouse
1008 Pearl St.
Ypsilanti, Mich. 48197

HOO'S KOIN BOX

This is based on the famous Okito box used by the magician of that name (in reality Theo Bamberg, who came from a family of magicians). However, the original has been altered so much that it is no longer clear exactly who should get the credit, so the new version was named, like the baseball player in the famous Abbott and Costello routine, after the man "who" was responsible. Hoo invented it? Right! Who uses it? You will—when you see what it can do.

Three half-dollar coins and one Chinese coin (with a hole in the center) vanish from the box while held in the hands of a spectator. The coins are found under the table.

A half-dollar is placed inside and a magic wand goes right through it—or use a pencil. Put a Chinese coin inside and it appears threaded on the wand.

The box is filled with coins and placed on the back of the hand, and the coins are seen up until the last split-second. Then they vanish, penetrate the hand, and fall onto the table.

Like it so far? There's more! The box is filled with coins and wrapped in a handkerchief. The four corners of the hanky are held together, with the box inside. The four coins vanish from the box and fall into a glass. The box is shown empty.

Two coffee cups are shown empty, and one is used to cover the box. Coins vanish from the box and appear in the other coffee cup, even though they were seen inside right up to the last second.

Three half-dollars and a Chinese coin are placed into the box. The Chinese coin penetrates the hand and is put back in the box. Now the three silver coins penetrate the hand and the Chinese coin is found under the table or wherever you like.

The box, Chinese "cash" coin, and special coins of other kinds needed for the above routine are all provided. The metal box has a hole in the top and the bottom so you can see the coins inside, and penetrate them with a pencil or wand. You will be able to perform countless other routines with this dynamite apparatus.

$30

Paul's Magic and Fun Shop
903 N. Federal Hwy.
Searstown, Fort Lauderdale, Fla. 33304

5 | ESCAPE MAGIC

Houdini. The name itself seems magic. But did you know that the famous and fabulous king of escapes and illusions started his career as a card expert? He not only spent his lifetime perfecting incredible feats to amaze the world, but he spent many years exposing fake mediums and fortunetellers whom he felt would discredit his profession. He was interested in everything magic, and his influence in the world of illusion is felt by all those who have followed him.

Yet, nowhere is his influence as strongly felt as in the area of escapes. He invented hundreds of them, and most were so miraculous that to this day there are people who believe he could dematerialize, float outside his shackles, and then return to his physical body.

The truth is all the more remarkable, because he could not rely on supernatural powers. He simply was a genius. Harry Houdini escaped from a Siberian prison van that was welded shut. He escaped from jail cells, from handcuffs, from straitjackets, and from bags, boxes, and ropes. He escaped from milk cans filled with water that were so small he could barely squeeze his body in. He escaped from a water torture cell that was a tank in which he was suspended head first in almost 2,000 gallons of water. The list is endless, as is his renown.

Escapes are probably the most dramatic form of magic, because to achieve recognition and fame such as that of Houdini calls for special abilities—dexterity, strength and stamina, intelligence and resourcefulness, and, in some cases, courage. To be like Houdini is to flirt with danger and court disaster. More than half a century after his death, his greatest feats are still unexplained, still unduplicated. But, Houdini-like effects can be achieved with the many exceptional effects available to magicians today.

HOUDINI'S PILLORY ESCAPE

A large wooden pillory is shown and then allowed to be examined. When the top bar is lifted,

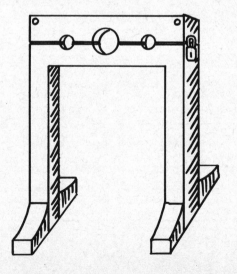

the magician rests his neck and wrists in the holes. The top is put back into place and locked securely. A screen is placed in front and the magician escapes easily.

$400

Healey's Magic Co.
1612 Dickson Ave.
Scranton, Pa. 18509

NITE-CLUB VANISH

A table is shown, draped to cover all four sides. An assistant steps up on the table and stands in the center of a bag. The magician gets up on the table and pulls the bag over the assistant's head. He steps down, fires a shot, and lets the bag drop flat. When asked where to look, audience yells "Under the table!" The front drape is drawn off to show the empty space. This is a very lovely vanish that can be done with spectators surrounding the table.

$550

Healey's Magic Co.
1612 Dickson Ave.
Scranton, Pa. 18509

RED TAPE THUMB TIE

For many years mediums devised elaborate tricks to convince people that spirits were working with them. One of the most common tricks was to have someone tie the medium up. The "thumb tie" is one of the most famous methods.

It's foolproof and can be performed immediately without long practice. Everyone knows how sticky Scotch tape is and how well it binds. In this case, the tape is used to bind the thumbs together. The trick is to have an assistant pass wooden hoops through your tightly bound thumbs, or to have a volunteer hold a cane at both ends while you push it through your taped thumbs so your hands are locked on the other side of it—just as if they had not been taped at all!

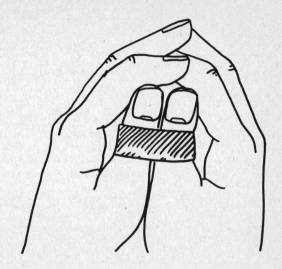

The method used is so ingenious you'll marvel at it. The routines included will let you astound your audience.

$5

Healey's Magic Co.
1612 Dickson Ave.
Scranton, Pa. 18509

SIBERIAN CHAIN ESCAPE

A nickel-plated chain with lock is passed out for examination. The performer permits spectators to chain his wrists, explaining to the audience that if they will time him he will escape from chains in five seconds. The performer turns his

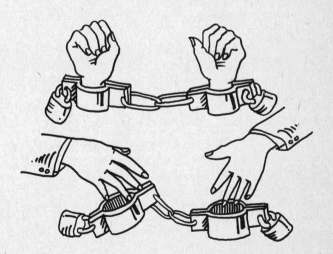

back and does a Houdini-like escape. He is out of the chains in two seconds. Chain and lock can then be handed out once more to show they are intact and not tampered with. This is an excellent trick for parlor or stage.

$2

Warner's Magic Factory
Box 455
Hinsdale, Ill. 60521

SHANGHAI SHACKLE

Here is an escape trick that is ridiculously easy to do, and will be all the more effective for that.

Two long ropes are threaded through a heavy tube and looped back through two holes in the ropes. The magician's hands are put through the rope loops. The ends of the ropes are held taut and the ends of the rope exchanged and tied. Volunteers, holding the ends, may pull as hard as they wish. The ropes penetrate the magician's wrists and the tube, and he is instantaneously released whenever he wishes to be. The tube falls free to the floor. Everything can be examined at once because there is nothing to hide.

$6.50

Jose's Studio
17-C Wallace St.
Belleville, N.J. 07109

THE SUBSTITUTION TRUNK

A strong trunk is brought onstage, where it can be examined by an audience committee. The performer's assistant is locked in handcuffs and is placed inside the trunk, which is then securely locked. A curtain is brought forward and placed around the trunk. The magician steps behind the curtain and on the count—one, two, three—the curtains are opened to reveal the assistant. The trunk is then unlocked and opened to show the magician has miraculously appeared inside the trunk locked in handcuffs. This illusion was made famous by the great Houdini, who featured it in his act with his wife Bess.

This is a beautiful custom-made trunk, built to last a lifetime, which features beautiful two-tone natural wood finish and heavy cloth lining. This trunk is pictured with Capo and Company.

$750

James Swoger, House of Enchantment, Inc.
Lake Road, R.D. 7
Somerset, Pa. 15501

ESCAPE IRONS

Perform impossible Houdini-like escapes. Hand-crafted "irons" of heavy stainless steel are gimmicked for easy release when you know their secret even with a lock furnished by the audience. The "irons" are joined by heavy 1-inch chain links and the neck collar has a 3-foot chain which allows you to lock it to your wrist and ankle.

Wrist bracelet $15
Ankle bracelet $15
Neck collar $12.50

Zanadu
165 Hancock Ave.
Jersey City, N.J. 07307

WEINER THUMB TIE

Here's an Irv Weiner masterpiece almost anyone can perform with the assurance of a professional. No long practice necessary, yet the escape is foolproof and more baffling than any other similar trick because everyone knows what Scotch tape is and how well it binds. In this case, it is used to bind your thumbs together, in a method so ingenious you'll marvel at it yourself as those wooden hoops pass onto your arms right through your tightly bound thumbs. Or pass your tightly bound hands through a cane held at both ends by a spectator or through the rungs of a chair, etc.

$5

Irv Weiner
1236 Great Plain Ave.
Needham, Mass. 02192

GIRL IN THE PLASTIC BAG

As you unfold this huge plastic bag you explain that your assistant will escape from it. She makes her entrance wearing a brief outfit, and with your aid and that of a volunteer from the audience, steps into the bag. You and the volunteer then seal the top of the bag with ordinary paper masking tape. A large cloth is held in front as you explain that she has only a limited time to get out because of the lack of air inside.

Suddenly, the cloth is dropped, and she stands onstage free of the bag, which is still sealed—with her costume inside! She now wears a short bathrobe or cover. The bag can be inspected before and after. No trap doors—you can do this escape in your living room. Comes with two bags, each of which can be used several times.

$6

Lou Tannen
1540 Broadway
New York, N. Y. 10036

TRIPLE ESCAPE MYSTERY

A dynamite illusion allowing the artist to escape from a well-built cabinet that will bear the closest inspection. Inside, a series of double cleats at sides—three shelves divide at the middle to provide openings just large enough to secure performer at neck, waist, wrist, and ankles. Front parts of shelves are removed to allow performer to step into cabinet and then are replaced. Each shelf is chained and padlocked by volunteers. Front door is then closed and locked on the outside, making escape seemingly impossible. Performer escapes in less time than it took to secure him.

$700

Healey's Magic Co.
1612 Dickson Ave.
Scranton, Pa. 18509

SACK ESCAPE

A very simple and elegant escape from a cloth sack. The sack is examined before the magician climbs in and the top is tied with ropes. A screen is placed around the sack and the magician promptly escapes.

$50

Healey's Magic Co.
1612 Dickson Ave.
Scranton, Pa. 18509

HANDCUFF ESCAPES AND MORE!

This is a truly amazing escape. This magic kit provides handcuffs, keys, and also two picks. In addition, a full escape pamphlet is provided that teaches you to pick cuffs and open locks while onstage! It's a tested and proved routine.

$7.50

Zanadu
165 Hancock Ave.
Jersey City, N.J. 07307

HANDCUFF ESCAPE

Escape tricks are fairly rare compared with many other kinds of illusions, and they always bring a lot of applause and amazement. A pair of regulation ratchet handcuffs are handed around for examination, and you can safely defy anyone to find anything wrong with them. They can be snapped on a spectator's wrist, and even with the key he will find it impossible to free himself.

But when the cuffs are snapped on your wrists, a volunteer can keep the key, seal the keyholes, and still, in a few seconds' time, you are out. The seals on the cuffs will be intact. The escape can be repeated immediately and performed anywhere. Everything necessary is included.

$22.50

Lou Tannen
1540 Broadway
New York, N.Y. 10036

HOUDINI PILLORY ESCAPE PLANS

The performer invites a committee to come up from the audience and examine an old-fashioned pillory made of solid materials. It stands 5 feet high and more than 3 feet wide and seems both strong and substantial.

Any volunteer—no assistant is required—can lock the performer's head and hands in place, and yet when the performer is screened from view he can escape immediately. Again, the entire apparatus can be examined.

Workshop plans.

$2

Lou Tannen
1540 Broadway
New York, N.Y. 10036

AUSTRALIAN BELT AND MUFF

This is as sensational as the straitjacket escape and quite different from anything most spectators have ever seen. The outfit consists of a wide full-grained leather belt that fastens in the back, with large leather loops and heavy chains and rings.

The arms and wrists are enclosed in the leather loops and securely fastened with the chains and padlocks. In a matter of seconds you can escape while standing in full view if you wish. There are no trick chains, locks, or buckles, so everything can be examined before and after your escape. Chains are chrome-plated. Complete instructions are included.

$27.50

Prynce E. Wheeler
P.O. Box 349
Great Falls, Mont. 59403

X-L SPIRIT TIE

This is a practical and very effective method of allowing your hands to be tied in a way that looks completely secure and escapeproof—yet allowing you to free your hands rapidly at will.

After your wrists are circled and bound tightly you can even have people try to pull your wrists apart. They will not break loose. Yet, you can free yourself in a matter of seconds under cover of a cloth or with your back turned.

Unlike the Kellar tie, you do not have to steal slack so that your wrists only seem to be tightly bound. This escape is fully explained and illustrated so that you can begin using it at once.

$2.50

Prynce E. Wheeler
P.O. Box 349
Great Falls, Mont. 59403

CROSS ESCAPE

A large wooden cross is shown. The performer is securely tied with ropes at neck, waist, and both wrists and the end of the ropes are held by volunteers. A curtain or screen is placed in front of the cross and is quickly lowered to reveal the cross standing empty. This is a very quick escape illusion. When ordering, include your height from floor to waist, and from waist to neckline. Also give the distance from wrist to wrist as measured across your chest with your arms spread wide.

$300

Healey's Magic Co.
1612 Dickson Ave.
Scranton, Pa. 18509

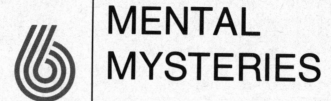

6 MENTAL MYSTERIES

The acceptance of ESP as a respectable field of scientific inquiry is probably directly responsible for a renewed interest in mentalism—the magic of clairvoyance, telepathy, precognition. Or is it magic? Perhaps the fascination is all the greater because the spectator can never be absolutely certain if the magician is performing a trick or if he or she really has special powers—ESP.

The most famous of the mentalists, the late Joseph Dunninger, amazed society in the 1930s with his impressive mindreading demonstrations that he presented as real. In the 1950s he was able to enthrall the nation through the growing medium of television. But, like Houdini, when he died his startling effects died with him.

Unlike Houdini, he has his successors, such as the Amazing Kreskin, who performs fabulous mental feats and tells how he does them ... sometimes. Or Jack London and Al Karan, who think of themselves as showmen. But what about Uri Geller? He claims his powers to bend keys are mental and real while magicians admit to doing the same thing by trickery.

Uri Geller might be genuine—but perhaps not all the time. The mentalist may be a trickster—but he or she could have special powers. Exciting possibilities are opening up in pyschic studies, and the Rhine experiments at Duke have

4.00

the buckley trilogy

GEMS OF MENTAL MAGIC

BY
Arthur Buckley

been accepted as scientific, even if the results have only been limited.

In mentalism, the ways of producing seeming miracles are almost never-ending. But the way to make those miracles seem real is to avoid using anything that looks like magical apparatus. In fact, the tools of your performance should be the same as the tools of the scientific experiments. There are special ESP cards, slates, and other everyday props. And perhaps the best advice for the performing mentalist is to learn a lesson from your audience—keep an open mind. Develop your skills and you might discover the trick is that ESP is not a trick at all.

PREDICTROLA PERFORMED BY DUNNINGER AND YOU

Here is a combination of a knockout display of mentalism, spiritualism, and nostalgia that produces a classic in close-up entertainment. You are given credit for joining forces with the one and only Dunninger in a truly professional presentation.

The performer introduces a cassette player and places it in plain view. A small box containing nine printed cards and a cassette is removed from the performer's pocket. The cassette is inserted in the player and the pile of cards is laid on the table.

While going through these procedures, the performer explains that he was a close associate of Dunninger, the famed mentalist. Dunninger had sent him the cassette, the cards, and a personal letter explaining an unusual prediction, an experiment in mental perception. The prediction will succeed only if the performer (you) can perceive by instinct the proper time and place the prediction was made for. The performer now announces that he feels this is it. He has sensed it all day. He feels he has a mental rapport with the spirit of Dunninger.

The cassette recording is now started. The opening to Dunninger's past radio show is heard, followed by a message from Dunninger

explaining that memories of the past have a strange bearing on future events. The nine cards are titled with the names of nine famous programs out of the golden past of radio. Dunninger directs the performer to spread the cards out on the table and pick an assistant from the audience. Following Dunninger's instructions, the assistant chooses and eliminates programs (cards) one at a time. As each program is eliminated, its opening theme is actually heard. One program is left, and Dunninger confirms his prediction by correctly naming that card. At this time a ball of paper which has been in full view of the audience is opened to reveal the prediction in writing. An astounding conclusion to a remarkable walk down memory lane.

You receive the following:

1.—A high-quality cassette selected for long reliable service. It comes in its own unbreakable box, and the sound quality is very good throughout for the type of recordings included.

2.—Nine printed business-size cards that give the impression that they must have come from Dunninger.

3.—Dunninger's recorded narration of the effect. Dunninger, as you know, was the greatest mentalist of all time, and a professional of the highest degree. Selective and critical, he chose to give this effect his personal endorsement and talents. Authenticity and realism were a must for this presentation. The recording was actually made in Dunninger's home with a professional cassette recorder, and there is a $1000 reward for anyone that can prove this is not the voice of Dunninger. Destined to become a collector's item.

4.—The opening radio themes include *Dunninger, Inner Sanctum, Charlie McCarthy, The Lone Ranger, Fred Allen, Terry and the Pirates, The Shadow, Amos 'n Andy, Gangbusters,* and *The Whistler.* These openings were selected for their mass popularity and for being unique in their melodic and audio effects. Absolutely fascinating even to those new to old-time radio.

$10

Gary C. Dudash
110 Montgomery Ave.
North Babylon, N.Y. 11704

SYMBOLISTIC

The magician requests the aid of two spectators. The first one chooses a card from a shuffled ESP pack—the *same* cards used in official ESP tests by Dr. J. B. Rhine at Duke University.

The second volunteer chooses a number that is counted onto a board that shows all five ESP symbols in a checkerboard pattern. The symbol arrived at is the same one as the symbol on the freely chosen card!

For greater impact an envelope that was in view of the audience at all times is opened, and it contains a prediction that also matches. The whole effect can be repeated immediately.

Besides the official ESP cards (you can use them to test yourself and your friends), you also get a heavy-duty plastic laminated board and complete instructions.

$10

Creative Magic Products
786 Merrick Rd.
Baldwin, N.Y. 11510

JACK LONDON'S BILLET READING ACT

Almost everyone who claims to be a medium or to have means to contact spirits uses the reading and answering of questions as a "test" of their powers. They call these "billets," from the French word for "note." You can do the same effect.

Distribute papers to the audience, requesting that each person write a question and sign his or her name to it. The folded slips are gathered in a hat by a volunteer and brought to the stage. Mix the slips, read an inspirational message from a book, and then reach into the hat and remove a question.

Hand the slip to a volunteer to hold, so that your hands are seen to be empty. The volunteer returns the slip to the writer, who can see it is his or her question while you answer it. This is repeated until the end of the act.

A few props are needed, but you can buy them yourself for about $2. This routine is extremely clever and comes to you in the form of a small booklet.

$3.50

Jack London
1937A Barnes Ave.
Bronx, N.Y. 10462

CHEATING THE GALLOWS

Maurice Fogel is one of the most stunning mentalists working today, though he is seldom seen in this country. Fogel performs such astounding tricks that even magicians often find themselves wondering if he is not using some ESP. One of his best effects, full of laughter and excitement, begins with the audience staring in fascination at a massive-looking gallows on stage. A committee of five volunteers is invited to examine the rope nooses used. There are five nooses—four are genuine and lethal; the fifth one has a snap fastener that will fall apart when pulled. Each rope is slipped into a cardboard cover so they all look alike.

The spectators mix up the ropes and hang them along a stand. One rope is chosen for the gallows. When the magician cannot obtain volunteers, he climbs up on a chair himself to test the noose. If all goes well and he has influenced the volunteers, by telepathy, to pick the right noose, he will be around for the applause. If not . . . He slips his head through the noose and jumps.

The rope parts, and he takes his bow to tremendous and well-deserved applause. What is offered here is the complete routine with full instructions and a construction plan for the gallows, which can be taken apart for easy packing. Book is fully illustrated and includes photos of the author in action.

Performing rights are included as well as a certificate that can be handed out to an audience member qualifying him or her as "A First Class Hangman."

$5

Glenn Comar
353 E. Sixth Ave.
Roselle, N.J. 07203

MENTAL SPOTS

Three cards, each with a different-colored spot, are removed from a transparent sleeve. The sleeve and the cards have a hole through their centers. Three ribbons with colors matching the cards are also used.

A spectator is asked to choose a colored ribbon while the magician places one of the cards in the sleeve. The spectator inserts the ribbon of his choice through the hole in the sleeve. When the card and ribbon are removed, the colors on the card and ribbon match!

Mental spots, the creation of El Duco, includes cards, ribbons, sleeve, and instructions.

$3

Accent Products
1550 West Dr.
Walled Lake, Mich. 48088

VOODOO DOLLS

Start your performance with a story about buying souvenir voodoo dolls on a recent trip. Invite a member of the audience to assist, seating him or her on a chair onstage. When you push a pin into one of the voodoo dolls, the volunteer jumps high in the air.

Then the volunteer is given one doll while you turn from him or her to push a pin into a second doll in full view of the audience. The volunteer is asked to stick a pin in his doll anywhere he likes. When the dolls are compared, the pins are both in the same position.

$6

Glenn Comar
353 E. Sixth Ave.
Roselle, N.J. 07203

MIRACLE MEMORY

A volunteer from the audience lists thirty to fifty words called at random by spectators. The words are numbered, then spectators call out the word

1. HOUSE   5. PECAN
2. OYSTER   6. SOUP
3. INK   7. COW
4. SPOON   8 WALLET

and you give its number, or they call the number and you supply the word.

Everything is written down out of your sight. Although the entire trick is done by memory, this method makes it so easy, so quick, and so sure that you can try it at once.

$1

Flosso Hornmann
304 W. 34th St.
New York, N.Y. 10001

ALMOST REAL PREDICTION

Ask any three spectators to assist you. Number one is asked to remove any bill from his or her wallet. Number two is asked to bring out his or her social security card, and number three writes any phone number that he or she desires on a pad of paper. Ask for two or three volunteers to guard and check your prediction of a total on the three items, making sure they see the numbers when you give it to them!

To save time you will work with the first four numbers on each of the three items. The spectator assistants are requested to call these numbers out, one digit at a time. You write the digits down on a large board in columns and the audience adds them up. The committee reads your prediction aloud, and it is 100 percent correct.

Other effects are possible with this remarkable principle. For example, you can predict the total of numbers chosen from cards in a face-up pack. Or the audience can call out any numbers to be used, yet you still predict the total.

$10

Jack London
1937A Barnes Ave.
Bronx, N.Y. 10462

SEALED ENVELOPE ACT

Actually answer the question in the envelope you hold in the air—and prove it!

Spectators write questions on cards, seal them in envelopes, and place their initials on the outside of the envelopes for positive identification. The envelopes are collected, dropped into a basket or a box, and mixed. Remove one envelope and read the initials, then show both sides of the envelope to the audience, holding it in the air while you answer the question inside. As you finish a question, discard the envelope in a box or, more dramatically, in a bowl of flames.

At any time open any envelope to prove you are answering the question that is in it. Props needed are an ordinary box or basket, scissors, blank business cards, and opaque envelopes.

$5

Jack London
1937A Barnes Ave.
Bronx, N.Y. 10462

TOP SECRET

Now, the perfect headline prediction, plus scores of other predictions of past, present, and future, thanks to this wonderful trick!

You can mail the predictions. You can seal the

predictions in anything, even a transparent box where they can be seen at all times.

You do not switch the prediction or use plants. Even at the time of reading you never go near or touch it.

Top secret eliminates the element of chance, the possibility of a slipup or exposure.

$2

Warner's Magic Factory
Box 455
Hinsdale, Ill. 60521

X-RAY EYES

This is without doubt one of the most wonderful demonstrations of clairvoyance ever presented. The medium's eyes are covered with large pieces of cotton wadding so that vision is completely cut off. The cotton is then sealed over the eyes with broad adhesive strips. As a further precaution, a heavy bandage is placed over the eyes and tightly tied around the head. Notwithstanding these restrictions, the medium successfully carries out a series of tests that seem unexplainable unless the medium is gifted with the faculty of clairvoyance. Chairs, lighted candles, goblets, handkerchiefs, and other obstructions are placed in any position about the stage by anyone, yet the medium's clairvoyant vision enables him or her to dance freely about and among these objects without disturbing them in the least. The medium quickly picks out articles, colors, numbers, cards named by the spectators. In conclusion, the medium goes into the audience and completely describes spectators, or articles, reads business cards, etc. All these tests are performed with the same speed and accuracy as though the medium had normal vision.

The act puzzles and holds the spectators' interest from start to finish.

$1

Warner's Magic Factory
Box 455
Hinsdale, Ill. 60521

MODERN TIMES MAGAZINE TEST

A printed typewriter prediction on a business-size card is placed in full view on a table. A spectator takes an ordinary issue of *Reader's Digest* and selects a page number between 50 and 100. A second person selects a number. Together the spectators turn to the selected page and look at the word in the first column that corresponds to the number decided on.

The typewritten prediction is read aloud by a third spectator:

"I predict volunteer number one will call out page ——; volunteer number two will choose the number four. The fourth word over on the fourth line of page —— will be ——."

The actual words in the blanks are written in longhand. This is direct magic that fools everyone. Walter Gibson, a magic authority who has written books for Thurston, Blackstone, and Houdini, says this is "the greatest I have ever seen. You may quote me."

$5

Aladdin Magic Shop
110 S. High St.
Columbus, Ohio 43215

MAIL MENTALISM

This trick is so incredible it is almost impossible even to explain what happens! You are not present. You need not even be in the same country. You don't have to see the deck or know the person or have any idea when the trick is being performed.

Write a letter to someone giving them instructions to do this card trick, or you can broadcast the instructions to a million families. It does not matter. The trick works every time. Even with a tape recording of the instructions, or with your letter in full view, the trick won't be revealed.

Instructions call for a deck of cards to be shuffled, one card selected, then put back in the deck. Applying the magic formula you send them, the card can be pulled every time. The formula is your own name!

It's hard to believe it but it works time after time.

$5

Abbott's Magic Co.
Colon, Mich. 49040

SUPREME MIND MASTER

Write a prediction on a slate or a piece of paper that is left in full view of the audience. Shuffle a deck of cards and cut, handing them to a volunteer, who continues to mix the cards while holding them in his own hands.

Ask the volunteer to remove six cards and to spread them face down. As the volunteer thinks of each of the cards, you name it. Each card is set aside as you call it out. After five cards have been eliminated, only one is left. Point out that this one card has been left until last by the assistant—not you. Ask him or her to concentrate on the card, which you not only name but which you show is the card you predicted.

This is a very mystifying display of psychic powers you'll find easy to do and possible to perform close-up. You do not have to switch your prediction.

$3

Abbott's Magic Co.
Colon, Mich. 49040

SPIRIT BELL

The magician or mindreader shows a small bell mounted on a tripod, and a large glass. They can actually be passed for close examination. The bell is then covered by the glass, turned upside down, and placed on a table or held in the hand.

Go through the audience picking up cards with numbers on them, questions, etc. Or have audience members choose a card from a pack. Or combine with a "billet reading" of questions in sealed envelopes. The possibilities are endless.

Still covered by the glass, the bell rings, indicating the selected cards by ringing the number of spots. Written numbers are indicated in the same manner, and it answers questions by ringing once for yes and twice for no.

The spirit bell is self-contained and does not require threads, wires, assistants, or secret co-operation from someone in the audience. It is entirely mechanical but detection is impossible. A riotous lie-detector routine that can be used with the spirit bell is included. The bell, by the way, rings in a loud and clear manner.

$42.50

Lou Tannen
1540 Broadway
New York, N.Y. 10036

HOROSCOPE WALLET PADS

It seems that everyone is interested in astrology these days, even if they wonder what the great attraction is for everyone else. And everyone seems to know the astrological sign (sun sign) he was born under. This effect uses the signs of the zodiac in an interesting new way.

Show the audience a square pad printed with the signs of the zodiac. Ask a spectator to remove one sheet and write his or her birthday on it along with some other item—a name, a color, a number, etc.—before folding the sheet over twice. The paper is torn into pieces and burned. You then write the birthdate and the other named item on a piece of paper, apparently reading the mind of the spectator. You also give the major character traits for that sign.

No carbons are used, no duplicates, no switching of papers. This is easy to do. The pad is attractive, and you get enough printed sheets for more than 140 performances.

$2

Jose's Studio
17-C Wallace St.
Belleville, N.J. 07109

UTISSAMO

The magician asks two spectators each to think of a card. He writes his guesses with a marking pen on blank-faced cards and places the cards in a rack in full view of the audience. Now the mentalist produces an ordinary deck of cards

and asks the spectators to please announce the cards they thought of. These cards are removed from the deck and placed in the rack. The magician's impressions are seen to match the selected cards.

The card rack revolves and is made of gleaming black and clear Lucite.

$13.50

Creative Magic Products, Inc.
786 Merrick Rd.
Baldwin, N.Y. 11510

LITE TOUCH

Here is a stunning effect, not just mindreading but an entirely new form of miracle. Ask a spectator to choose a card. Ask a second spectator to stare into the flame of a match so that the name of the card is revealed to them. The person whom you choose is an ordinary member of the audience, not someone to whom you have given special instructions. The necessary materials are right there in full view of all the spectators, but only one person perceives the chosen card while looking through the light of the match.

This is a very clever principle and is extremely easy to do. Another effect—very different from the first one—is also possible. You claim it is possible to see through a book of matches. To prove it, you place a book of matches on the back of a card. A spectator first sees nothing. Next he sees the card's suit. Next he sees the value of the card. You don't have to suggest anything—he really gets the information in that order.

Instructions and those "special somethings" are included.

$2

Jose's Studio
17-C Wallace St.
Belleville, N.J. 07109

ESP BRAINWASHED

A deck of ESP cards is given to a spectator. From behind his back he selects any one of the twenty-five ESP cards. This card is held sight unseen—nobody, neither spectator, nor audience, nor performer, knows what this card is (absolute free choice).

From a second pack of ESP cards you remove five cards of a set. These five cards are placed backs facing the audience. Now four different spectators choose a card (free choice) one at a time. Only one card is left.

This card is turned over, and the first card chosen by the spectator is now turned over. They match! No stooge or helper at any time.

$2.50

The Jokers Wild
Box 513
Cape Coral, Fla. 33904

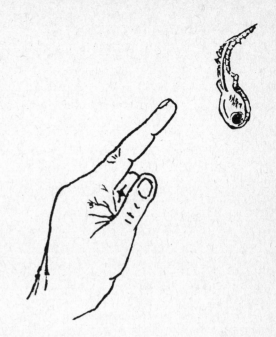

THREE VINYL SLEEVES

Three vinyl sleeves containing three blue-backed playing cards are placed before the spectator. The sleeves have a die-cut window and are cut shorter than the cards, so the cards are visible at all times.

A red-backed deck is shuffled and shown front and back to be normal. With the red deck face up, the spectator points to any card. The card is removed from the deck by the magician.

The spectator now selects any of the three vinyl sleeves. The performer places the red card in the selected sleeve. While holding the sleeve, the performer requests the spectator to remove the red and blue cards from the sleeve. The red and blue cards bear identical faces!

The other vinyl sleeves are turned over to show that they contain different cards than the one chosen by the spectator. If desired, three blue cards can be chosen and each card inserted into one of the sleeves. All red and blue cards will match!

$6

Accent Products
1550 West Dr.
Walled Lake, Mich. 48088

KEYBENDER

Ever since Kreskin bent his first key this has been the sign of a great mentalist. This is in our opinion the best of the key-bending effects available. No apparent props, no sleights—almost self-working.

Keys are borrowed, and while stroking one in your hand, it actually bends. Your hands never approach your body. No switches or gimmicks to get rid of. You are always ready and everything may be examined.

$5

Richard Mark
14600 S.W. 63rd Ct.
Miami, Fla. 33158

SPIRIT PEN

This is one of the most baffling effects ever released—a trick the audience will remember for a long time. A handkerchief is borrowed and a ball-point pen is introduced and wrapped up in the handkerchief. This is given to a spectator to hold. Next the performer shuffles a deck of cards and has one chosen by the spectator. The card is replaced in the deck and shuffled. The performer tells the spectator to concentrate on his card and then to unwrap the handkerchief. When the hanky is opened, the name of the card is written in ink on the handkerchief. The name of the card is written in longhand and there is positively no trace as to how the writing got there.

$3.50

Magicraft Products
P.O. Box 2392
North Canton, Ohio 44720

EIGHT-CARD BRAINWAVE

One of the most subtle mental secrets in magic today! Anyone in the audience simply calls out the name of any card of eight different cards that you display. You then show all the backs, and the named card is a different color than the others!

$2.50

The Jokers Wild
Box 513
Cape Coral, Fla. 33904

ESP CHIPS

The performer places several deluxe thick chips on the table. Each chip has different ESP symbols engraved into both faces of the chip. A prediction is written and given to a spectator for safekeeping.

The spectator is asked to stack the chips. When the stack is completed, the symbols on the top and bottom of the stack match the written prediction! The effect can be immediately repeated with a different conclusion.

$10

Accent Products
1550 West Dr.
Walled Lake, Mich. 48088

MIRACLE MATCH

The magician exhibits five vinyl sleeves. On the back of each sleeve is a printed ESP symbol. On the front of each sleeve is a transparent window. An ESP card is seen inside the window, and the design on the card matches the design printed on the sleeve. The performer removes the five cards, allowing the sleeves to be seen empty. The five cards are turned face down, mixed, and spread before the spectator. The sleeves are also spread out with the printed symbols showing.

The spectator is asked to guess which card matches which sleeve. The magician slips each card selected by the spectator into each sleeve specified by the spectator. When all five cards have been inserted, the sleeves are turned over. The spectator has matched the five pairs of symbols! The cards can now be removed so the sleeves can be seen empty. The sleeves are mechanical and do the work for you.

$8.50

Accent Products
1550 West Dr.
Walled Lake, Mich. 48088

FANTASTIC MENTAL TEST

1.—Show a bowl containing slips of paper on which are written the names of cities. Someone picks up a dozen slips and gives one to you to seal in an envelope. You then name the city.

2.—A borrowed bill is sealed in an envelope. You are able to name the serial number.

3.—People write out tests for you to perform. One is selected and sealed in an envelope, yet you are able to do as instructed.

With this little booklet you are basically getting the professional technique actually used in Jack London's act.

$3.50

Jack London
1937A Barnes Ave.
Bronx, N.Y. 10462

NOW'S YOUR CHANCE

At your request a volunteer from the audience writes a prediction. Other spectators write digits on a piece of paper—any digits they choose. These are added up by anyone, or can be called out, written on a blackboard, and added. The total matches exactly the prediction made by the volunteer.

These are not members of your staff, but strangers, and there is no switch of papers, digits, or cards. This can be done as a prediction or as a clairvoyance test in which you receive impressions by "psychic waves."

The effect is impressive, yet easy to do. You get two gold-finished ball-point pens and instructions.

$2.75

Jose's Studio
17-C Wallace St.
Belleville, N.J. 07109

CALCU-TOTAL

Something new in mentalism. This is a surefire effect that can be a feature item in any mental act. It is suited for an opening or closing effect, and is ideal for both stage and close-up work.

One spectator is handed a prediction and a second spectator is handed an electronic calculator. The spectator with the calculator is requested to punch in any four-digit number and then to add, subtract, multiply, or divide by any other four-digit number, doing this repeatedly until he or she wishes to stop. The answer to calculations matches prediction! The usual audience reaction after seeing this is stunned astonishment.

Once the calculator is handed to the spectator, the magician does not touch it.

This is one of many possible effects. The magician has full control over the final answer, making Calcu-Total ideal for use in "fairly" selecting a number for a book test, telephone-number force, etc.

Instructions give ideas for various effects, but you will come up with many more of your own.

Calcu-Total can also be used as a regular calculator, making this an extremely practical buy. Mailed first class insured.

$30

Sheldon Aronowitz
15–19 Parmelee Ave.
Fair Lawn, N.J. 07410

DY-NO-MITE PREDICTION

The performer makes a prediction (preferably of a newspaper headline) weeks before the long-awaited performance. It is mailed and brought to the stage on the night of the show by the appropriate person (district attorney, school principal, minister . . . the creditable person in charge). He verifies the postmark on the envelope sealed with sealing wax. He states that no one (including you) has so much as touched it since it has been in his possession. Now he breaks the wax seal and tears open the envelope. He takes out the prediction and he reads the prediction to the audience as you hold up a copy of that day's paper to thunderous applause. It's that simple! It can be notarized, too!

This trick uses no gimmicks or stooges at any time! No carbons or trick envelopes are involved. You do not touch the envelope or the prediction. It's in the hands of the person to whom it is mailed at all times. There are no switches made by anyone! It requires no practice and no sleights!

$10

Donn Davison
P.O. Box 80747
Atlanta, Ga. 30366

SIGHTLESS VISION

The blindfold act always baffles audiences everywhere. Members of the audience place a piece of cardboard over your eyes and then plaster it with putty or dough, and cover it with cotton and then adhesive tape. A blindfold is then placed over this and a black hood is placed over your head and tied around your neck. Yet with this super method, you can drive a car, write, duplicate numbers and names written on a blackboard, play pool, ride a bike, pick out colors, and do scores of other "impossible" feats.

Full instructions, including hood.

$10

Lou Tannen
1540 Broadway
New York, N.Y. 10036

CELESTIAL SLATE

A message appears on a blank slate. You show the slate blank on both sides, then wrap it in a sheet of newspaper and give it to a spectator to hold. When the spectator unwraps the slate, a message from the spirits is found to be on it.

This is good for use with spirit effects as well as for mindreading effects or for revealing a chosen card—which can be chosen after the slate is wrapped! Many other possibilities will occur to you.

You get the slate and the "flap" that makes all this possible.

$2.50

James Rainho Products
16 Windsor Rd.
Medford, Mass. 02155

MENTAL EPIC

Display a slate that is marked off into six equal squares and make three predictions in the top three spaces. Cover these up with three squares of cardboard.

The spectator puts his choices in the bottom three spaces, and your predictions match his! Any kind of item can be used—words, books, numbers, colors, designs, names, playing cards. Anything is possible with this—it belongs in the miracle class. No skill or effort required; it is all self-working.

$25

Abbott's Magic Co.
Colon, Mich. 49040

GRANT'S ESP

Two sets of ESP cards are shown. The first set is shuffled face down and the performer picks out two cards, which he puts in a clear plastic stand with the backs facing the audience.

The second set is fanned out face up and two spectators are each asked to call out a design. These two cards are placed in the stand beside the performer's cards. The two sets of cards match.

This is one of the most direct and mind-boggling ESP tests ever devised. The stand is 6×8 inches and is clear plastic with a chrome strip, very narrow, to hold the cards in place.

$3.75

House of Enchantment
Lake Rd., R.D. 5
Somerset, Pa. 15501

BLITZ!

Walk in with an unlit cigarette in one hand and a matchbox in the other. Strike a match on the box and nothing happens. Strike it again and then things really start to pop!

The match changes to a silk. The matchbox changes to three silks. Three more silks appear alongside the first one that appeared. Reaching into the midst of all these silks you bring out a full-sized glass of wine!

A special silk is included along with the glass and everything else that is needed to make things work right, but you have to supply six silks of your own.

$15

Samuel Berland
517 S. Jefferson St.
Chicago, Ill. 60607

PINNACLE SLATE

This is an astounding slate effect. The slate is blank, until words or messages you choose suddenly appear. This method defies examination. It can be used to obtain an unlimited number of effects without flaps or sliding parts. It uses an entirely new method of operation that is unlike anything else ever used to obtain magic slate writing.

$21

John Cornelius
430 Elmwood
San Antonio, Tex. 78212

ESP SPOTS

Here is a mindreading stunt that's spectacular. A large black domino, made of metal, comes with six magnetic spots. Invite a volunteer to come up and arrange the spots on the domino.

Then you take four cards and show that they are blank. Suddenly, spots appear on one of the cards—in the same combination as the volun-

teer has placed them on the domino. The other three cards are still blank. But look! The spots are printed on the card. There is no way that can happen, but it does. All the cards can be examined.

$8.50

Lou Tannen
1540 Broadway
New York, N.Y. 10036

PHONEY

The supreme mental effect, with no practice and no skill required. Someone opens a copy of your local phone book to any page and writes down a name and number from any column. The performer immediately identifies the chosen entry. All you need to perform this is a copy of your local phone directory and this instruction booklet.

$5

Glenn Comar
353 E. Sixth Ave.
Roselle, N.J. 07203

BOOK OF THE MIND

Here is a sensational mental mystery that works on an entirely new principle. Members of the audience select one of four bound books—or all four. The books are absolutely legitimate. A page from each book is freely chosen, and a word from the page is remembered. You then reveal each and every word, one at a time, by writing it in chalk on a small slate. You show the word before the volunteers reveal the word they selected. No questions are asked. No secret help is required—it's a one-person effect. Nothing is written by the spectators, and the books will stand examination.

$32.50

Lou Tannen
1540 Broadway
New York, N.Y. 10036

SPELLBOUND

A dramatic set of miracles from exotic India. You can apparently cause anyone to become spellbound—unable to stand, raise a gun, read.

Five big effects:

1.—Performer spellbinds a volunteer so that the person is unable to rise from a chair.

2.—Murder test. Volunteer is given a revolver and is unable to raise his arm to point it at the audience.

3.—Breeze of India. Volunteer stands facing you. You say a breeze from your finger tips is so strong he or she will fall backward. The volunteer falls.

4.—You apparently cause a volunteer to lose clear sight and become unable to read.

5.—A man is spellbound and is unable to walk over to a pretty girl and kiss her!

Use any subjects. This is trickery of the cleverest type—nothing scientific. *Anyone* can work these. These and five other great mysteries are included.

$1

Flosso Hornmann
304 W. 34th St.
New York, N.Y. 10001

7 | CREATING CLOSE-UP CONFUSION

What's close-up confusion?

A man comes up to you and pulls a half-dollar out of your ear. You open your mouth to complain and he pulls out an egg. It's a real one—he cracks it, and the yolk comes out. Before you can complain or exclaim or even get your breath back he asks you what time it is—but you can't tell him because your watch is on his wrist. Not only that, but somehow he has managed to get your necktie off, too.

And you thought you were wide awake.

At that point he puts a stack of quarters on the back of your hand and a moment later they change to dimes. He borrows a dollar and you tear a corner off one so you can recognize it again. He locks it in a tube, only when the tube is opened the dollar is gone. Where? To the inside of a lemon?

This is known as close-up magic. It's fun. The audience is often part of the act. The cynics can surround you and still never catch on to the tricks. Some of these effects are smooth enough for a night-club routine done as you stroll from table to table. Much of this magic is incredibly baffling wherever it is done.

Don't misunderstand—some of these mini-illusions only cost a dollar or two, but that doesn't mean they are anything except terrific.

Doug Henning's full evening musical, *The Magic Show*, was full of giant illusions, but the one thing that had even the cast baffled was a little item that could have been picked up for a few dollars—in a much smaller size—at any novelty shop. Presentation is all-important.

A lot of time and talent goes into inventing these effects, and whether they are small or large, close-up or requiring a stage, costly or inexpensive, the genius of the original inventor is what is being offered to you. Your performance, however, depends on your skills and showmanship. The magic ingredient in any show is the performer—you.

THE VANISHING ELEPHANT

Houdini used to make a giant pachyderm vanish from the middle of the stage. Six assistants would move a large cage onstage. A circus elephant would be led into the cage, and the cage would be covered by curtains. A loud drum roll, a sudden pistol shot, and the curtains fell to the floor. The elephant had vanished into thin air! Then more than a dozen roustabouts or sturdy helpers would take down the empty cage.

Wherever the elephant was, it certainly was not hidden behind one of the sections of cage to be secretly carried off on someone's shoulder!

Well . . . it was a trick, of course. Even Houdini couldn't afford the cost of a new elephant for every performance. Now you can avoid the supply problem and the price of upkeep and feed for a large animal with this miniature version of the elephant vanish.

A 2-inch solid plastic pachyderm is placed on a thin board that is not tampered with or faked in any way. You build a cage around the elephant with four vinyl cards that are also innocent. When you snap your fingers, the cage immediately collapses.

The elephant has dematerialized—as you proceed to demonstrate in a most uncanny manner. It's quick, different, mechanical, and easy to do.

$12.50

Lou Tannen
1540 Broadway
New York, N. Y. 10036

BAMBOO CHEST AND GLASS

A beautiful chest with Chinese design is displayed. A tall glass of water is placed inside and locked into the center of the chest so that it cannot move.

Four solid-chrome blades are pushed through the center from side to side. This leaves no space for the glass of water—yet it is still in there. Remove the pole and blades, open the front of the cabinet, and the audience will see the glass is still locked in place. It is removed and water is poured out.

Another close-up miracle! Beautiful apparatus, startling and unexplainable effect, and clever dialogue are all included.

$42.50

Aladdin Magic Shop
110 S. High St.
Columbus, Ohio 43215

FALL OUT

A plated washer and a steel ball are handed to the audience for examination. The spectators can readily see that the steel ball cannot pass through the hole in the washer. The washer is placed on top of a soda bottle and covered with a leatherette tube which fits snugly over the top of the bottle. A volunteer may look down in to see that the washer is still there. Drop the steel ball into the tube. It penetrates the washer and falls into the bottle!

Everything may be examined before and after. There is no switching!

$1

Warner's Magic Factory
Box 455
Hinsdale, Ill. 60521

HOUDINI VANISHES

This is a pocket-sized economy version of the Houdini water-torture cell. The real thing costs almost $10,000. In this case, the tiny magician, dressed in a black tuxedo, is only 2 inches tall. The clear plastic water-torture cell is 3 inches tall. The escape artist fits into the little cylindrical object head downward. Once he's inside, he remains in full view. You put the cap on, then offer the cylinder for inspection. When you hand the torture cell to a spectator, the magician has vanished!

At no time is there any other cover than your own fingers. The instructions are clearly written, and will make it possible to master this effect quickly.

$3

Jose's Studio
17-C Wallace St.
Belleville, N. J. 07109

JARDINE ELLIS RING

This is one of the great classics of close-up magic. The ring is large, heavy, and brass-colored. It can be threaded onto a stick held at both ends by a spectator. It can appear and reappear on the spectator's finger, or the ring can magically find its way off the ribbon it is strung on. Full routines are included.

$5

Glenn Comar
353 E. Sixth Ave.
Roselle, N. J. 07203

A SPLASH OF COLOR

This is brand-new and one of the easiest and most beautiful effects in magic. The many possibilities include:

1.—Think of a color. A glass of water dramatically changes color a few seconds after being poured.

2.—Think America. Clear water is poured into three glasses and its color changes to red, clear, and blue, representing the American flag.

3.—Think of a rainbow. Eight empty glasses are filled with clear water. The base of each glass is wrapped with a different-colored silk handkerchief. At the magician's command each glass of water changes into a different color, matching the silks!

This is an easy feat. You add nothing but water; no measurements are necessary. Colors can all be made "clear" again if you wish!

Think of a color $10
Think America $12.50
Think of a rainbow $25

The Wizard
1136 Pearl St.
Boulder, Colo. 80302

ULTRA BALLOON PENETRATION

A long balloon is inserted into a tube and inflated so that both ends of the balloon protrude beyond both ends of the tube. Two long, sharp knitting needles are pushed through holes on the side of the tube, and apparently right through the inflated balloon without damaging it.

Tube and balloon are shown all around for examination. The balloon is burst and the tube shown again, with the needles crisscrossed inside the tube. The needles are removed and everything can be examined.

$8

James Rainho Products
14 Windsor Rd.
Medford, Mass. 02155

VANISHING WHISKEY GLASS

An ordinary whiskey glass containing any kind of liquid is held in full view on palm of hand. Cover the glass with your other hand. Squeeze hands together, then open. Both hands are shown positively empty.

The same glass, not a duplicate, is produced from behind knee or from a spectator or anywhere your fancy dictates. Do it again immediately. No preparation is necessary.

$1

Warner's Magic Factory
Box 455
Hinsdale, Ill. 60521

CHINESE STICKS

Magician shows two 14-inch-long glittering sticks with cords and tassels dangling from the front ends. One stick has a short cord and the other a long one.

When the short cord is pulled the long one rises up and becomes short, and the short one becomes long. The cords rise in a most uncanny manner! This may be repeated as often as you wish.

$15

James Rainho Products
14 Windsor Rd.
Medford, Mass. 02155

IMMO, THE IMMORTAL CIGARETTE

Take an ordinary cigarette, break it in half, and hold a half in each hand. The torn ends are placed together and the cigarette becomes fully restored. The cigarette can then be smoked.

This unique method was granted a registration by the Magic Dealers Association. Only one cigarette is used. No extra halves or pieces are used.

$1.50

James Rainho Products
14 Windsor Rd.
Medford, Mass. 02155

AMAZERING

The magician borrows a finger ring from a spectator. The spectator then ties a loose knot in the center of a piece of rope and holds the ends. A hanky is draped over the knot and the magician picks up the ring and places it underneath the hanky, which is immediately pulled away. There is the ring, threaded on the rope and tied within the knot, which must be untied to remove the ring.

$4

James Rainho Products
14 Windsor Rd.
Medford, Mass. 02155

HANSEL AND GRETEL PAPER TEAM

A novel approach to a magic classic—the paper tear, with specially imprinted Hansel and Gretel that will make a big hit with your kid-show audiences! Tear up the picture and restore it . . . Ooops—you dropped the extra piece. Or did you? The dropped piece is opened up, and it's a picture of the wicked witch of the story! A finish to a great routine that usually gets a vocal response. Complete with lots of papers to do the trick over and over, plus three patter presentations to choose from. You'll have fun with this one—and your audiences will, too!

$3.50 postpaid.

Hank Lee's Magic Factory
24 Lincoln St.
Boston, Mass. 02111

RECORD MYSTERY

A genuine phonograph record is shown by the performer, who then places it in an attractive holder. The record is visible to the audience at all times. Now the performer takes a large knife and openly inserts it midway into the holder, slightly to one side of the record in place.

The impossible happens. The knife is pulled from one end of the holder to the other, apparently slicing right through the record—yet when the record is removed it is shown to be unharmed!

Only the one genuine record is used with any knife. It is not gimmicked. Attractive wooden holder, as pictured, packs flat.

$22.50

Micky Hades International
Box 2242
Seattle, Wash. 98111

DUSHECK'S WUNDERBAR

At last, you can now do a floating trick right under the noses of your audience.

A 2½-inch silver-colored metallic bar is freely shown inside a corked test tube. Suddenly it starts to jump around and pushes the cork out of the test tube. Then it leaves the test tube and floats from hand to hand. A real miracle.

You can carry Wunderbar in your pocket, always ready to perform anywhere, under all conditions. This was voted the best close-up trick of the year, so you know it's good.

$8.50

Steve Dusheck Jr.
1000 Seybert St.
Hazleton, Pa. 18201

THRU-BALL

Here is an eye-popping fooler that you can master five minutes after reading the directions. You display a glass and a small ball. You place the ball on top of the inverted glass, and easy as one-two-three the ball visibly penetrates the glass. This is clever and sure to fool any audience.

$3

Guaranteed Magic
27 Bright Rd.
Hatboro, Pa. 19040

TOMMY WINDSOR'S JUMBO PAPER FIR TREE

You show a roll of paper, make a couple of tears, and suddenly pull out a fir tree 14 feet tall. No switching. The paper is shown to be ordinary, yet it is gimmicked. This trick is easy to prepare and to perform but to the audience it appears as if it requires great skill. Instructions for a jumbo Jacob's ladder and for full color effects are also included free. Comes with a 4-page printed manuscript of instructions, tips, ideas, and patter (a full comedy routine by George McAthy) plus a sample paper. A surefire applause getter for you!

$3

Jacobs Productions
Box 362
Pomeroy, Ohio 45769

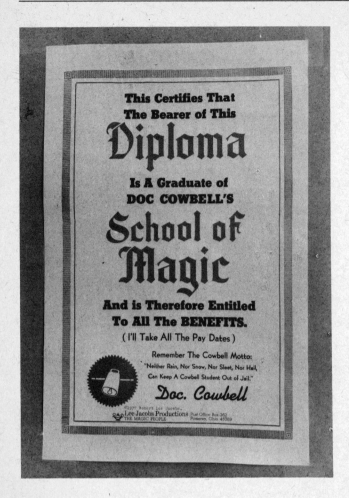

DIPLOMA TEARING TRICK

You explain that you went to magic school but flunked when you couldn't put the woman you sawed in half back together again. So, the professor tore up your diploma. But then you explain how you got back in the good graces of the professor and how he magically restored your diploma. You get the patter story that explains why they decided to tear up your diploma. And it is full of laughs. And you get enough of the beautiful, two-color, 11×17-inch diplomas printed from specially designed plates to do this hilarious trick fifteen times.

$5

Jacobs Productions
Box 362
Pomeroy, Ohio 45769

KAN'T TEAR PAPER

You'll certainly agree it's a lot of fun! One of the most outstanding fun effects that has come on the magic market for a long time. With each batch of special paper you get several audience-tested ideas that will create a great deal of laughter and enjoyment.

Show a piece of paper—it looks and feels like ordinary paper. Tear it in half and give a spectator one half. Ask him or her to tear it in half—but it can't be done! It seems as though all strength has gone from the spectator's fingers! Take the paper back and immediately tear it in half! This is fantastic fun in a kids' show! They twist and squirm in their efforts to tear the paper, but it can't be done. Only you can tear it! We give you a dozen of the special paper strips together with a selection of routines.

$2

Guaranteed Magic
27 Bright Rd.
Hatboro, Pa. 19040

NEW KOLORFUSING

Show a pocket knife (pen knife) that is red, and it suddenly changes to white. Change it back to red. Next, the knife is seen to be red at the top of your fist, and yet it immediately becomes white at the bottom of your fist. You can even do a slow visual change as you pass it through the fingers of your upturned hand. Then turn your hand upside down and the entire knife has changed color again. The knives can be examined.

You get three knives about 3 inches long, with a nickel-plated Swiss mirror finish and instructions. This is not for the beginner.

$12.50

Jose's Studio
17-C Wallace St.
Belleville, N.J. 07109

SMASH KNIFE CLIMAX

If you do a routine with pocket knives, this is a sensational climax. You put an ordinary-looking pen knife in your fist and smash it onto the table. It changes to a handful of tiny multicolored knives.

You get two dozen knives, which are ¾ inch long and have their blades open. These are in twelve different colors. You also get detailed instructions for using these in your act.

$5.50

Jose's Studio
17-C Wallace St.
Belleville, N.J. 07109

VISIBLE VAMPIRE

A large block (3¾ inches) with a hole through the sides is suspended from a chain. An open-front wood tube is shown to be empty (it really is empty, too). The block is lowered into the tube, where it remains in full view at all times. Holes in the sides of the tube line up with holes in the block, and a long wooden stake (a real stake) is pushed through the sides and extended beyond the outside of the tube. The block is impaled so no escape is possible.

And yet you pull the chain and the block visibly penetrates the stake and comes up out of the tube. This is a wonderful little miracle that can be done surrounded. There is only one block, it

is quite solid. The tube is more than a foot high, and the front of it is cut to look like a coffin.

$35

Aladdin Magic Shop
110 S. High St.
Columbus, Ohio 43215

PENETRA

A record can be carefully inspected and seen to be marked so that it cannot be changed. The magician shows a beautiful wooden stand on all sides, and sticks a large wooden or steel pen into a hole in its center. The stand is a solidly built equivalent of a paper record sleeve.

The record is put into the stand and the audience can see that the record rests on the pen. The magician says his magic formula, and slowly they see the record go though the pen. The top part of the stand is removed and the record can clearly be seen threaded on the pen.

Everything is completely automatic. Nothing is covered at any time, and when you remove the record and pen (or pencil) from the holder, it really is impaled through the center. You are even using a real record!

$45

Tom Fitzgerald
2814 Washington St.
Wilmington, Del. 19802

PHANTOM MYSTERY BLOCK

Here's another penetration that you'll like. It's an incredible pocket illusion.

A round block is shown and attention is drawn to the hole that runs through it. The block is placed into a round tube that also has two holes in it on opposite sides. A small metal rod is run through the tube and block, thus securing the block inside the tube. Slide the objects back and forth on the rod to show they are secured, then tap the top of the tube and the block falls from the rod. Thud! It lands on the table and the tube stays threaded on the metal rod. You don't believe it? Neither will they!

$2

Lou Tannen
1540 Broadway
New York, N.Y. 10036

MULTIPLYING PASSE-PASSE BOTTLES

There are many tricks that you can call sensational, but every magic dealer has only one trick he considers the best. Here is one that comes with that recommendation.

The multiplying passe-passe bottles are a new twist to an old classic. A bottle and a glass are placed on a table. These are each covered with a chrome tube. A magic formula is recited, the tubes removed, and the glass and bottle have changed places.

The effect is repeated: The bottle and glass are covered again, but when the tubes are removed a second bottle appears. The magician seems surprised and puts the second bottle aside. He covers the bottle and glass again and they change places as before. But again, when he attempts to repeat the effect, an extra bottle turns up and is set aside.

The magician finds himself producing bottles one after the other until the table top is filled with them. You get nine bottles and two chrome-finished tubes, plus complete instructions. This is a fine addition to a night-club act, or any other act where close-up magic is desired. Can be done surrounded. This is not only an impressive feat, but the apparatus is designed to last.

$35

Tom Fitzgerald
2814 Washington St.
Wilmington, Del. 19802

BLACK AND WHITE RABBIT PUZZLE

You have a pack of cards with a white rabbit in a black hat and another pack with a black rabbit in a white hat. A spectator sees one card from each pack, so there should not be a switch, but by turning the cards over they see the black rabbit in the black hat and the white rabbit in the white hat. You can do this close-up and use these as business cards, giving them away as souvenirs.

$2

Tom Fitzgerald
2814 Washington St.
Wilmington, Del. 19802

FLEXIBLE GLASS

Here is something new and different that everyone will know right away is completely impossible.

A model glass window is shown and proved to be real glass. It is then wrapped in a newspaper. The performer plunges a red dagger right through the center of the glass, and other holes are pierced at other places. Colored ribbons are threaded through the holes to show that they exist.

The performer states that under great strain, glass becomes flexible. Everyone knows better, but he proceeds to demonstrate that *his* glass has become flexible. He bends the wooden frame in half. There really is glass in the frame, yet it is bent back and forth as though it were soft plastic.

The paper is ripped off and the glass is found intact and solid as before.

$14.50

Lou Tannen
1540 Broadway
New York, N.Y. 10036

MUSIC FOR MAGIC

Everyone has handled 45-rpm records, but very few people have ever seen one behave the way yours does. You show a record and the little folder that it comes in, a brightly colored sleeve. The record may be examined. Push a ribbon through the hole in the folder and then push the record down into place. It goes right through the ribbon!

This is complete and self-contained, with a modern story for you to tell as you perform. It is a perfect opportunity for audience participation, and will have them truly puzzled.

$3

Lou Tannen
1540 Broadway
New York, N.Y. 10036

CONVINCING ROPE TRICK

After you have done a few rope tricks, this one is a good conclusion to that section of your program. The audience sees you cut the rope in two different places. The ends of each cut portion are tied. The rope is now in one length, with two knots in it where it was cut. You hold the rope in your fingertips in your right hand, and simply pass it through your left hand. It is miraculously restored to one piece and can be tossed out to the audience.

There is only one rope used—and it can be any piece of rope, because there is no preparation required. Further, no equipment is required to pull the rope up under your coat or switch it.

$5

Abbott's Magic Co.
Colon, Mich. 49040

BERLAND'S WATCH BAG

Magician Sam Berland has baffled other magicians at numerous conventions with the following incredible effect. He takes a cloth bag, turns it inside out—even invites someone to examine every stitch to prove that the bag is not a trick. Some coins, a cigarette lighter, and a watch that he borrows are dropped inside. The top of the bag is folded over and wrapped with a pocket handkerchief, and given to someone to hold.

The magician then announces that he is going to make everything in the bag penetrate right through the bag and handkerchief. He takes the bundle back from the spectator and bangs it on the table. Naturally, this makes a big hit with whoever lent the watch. "Now watch the articles come right through the cloth," says the performer. After a moment, when nothing happens, he decides where he went wrong.

The handkerchief is removed, the bag is in the same position as before, and the contents are spilled out. The coins fall out, and the lighter, and . . . no watch. Where is the borrowed watch? The magician pulls back his coat sleeve and reveals the watch on his own wrist! During the entire effect, everything has been scrutinized carefully. Not a single suspicious move has taken place. The method is sure and subtle. This can be done anywhere, even in a crowd where you are completely surrounded.

$6

Healey's Magic Co.
1612 Dickson Ave.
Scranton, Pa. 18509

MAGIC DRAWER BOX

It's shaped rather like a matchbox. The drawer slides in, the drawer slides out. You put cigarettes, pins, matches, coins, small silks, or other small items in and they vanish.

$1.50

Creative Magic Products
786 Merrick Rd.
Baldwin, N.Y. 11510

THE GREAT HINDU TURBAN MYSTERY

A length of soft white cloth is picked up. If you have been wearing it as a turban, then it is unwound. Or the cloth is produced, by the yard, in some preceding effect.

You have the cloth. Now, you get two members of the audience to come up and assist. They hold the cloth stretched between them. Then you take scissors and cut it through the center. The two pieces are tied together and the ends given to the two spectators so as to stretch the knotted cloth full length. You set fire to the knot, rub it between your hands, and the cloth is magically restored and pulled out full length for all to see and examine.

$2

Magic, Inc.
5082 N. Lincoln Ave.
Chicago, Ill. 60625

HUMAN HEN

This is very funny and can be used at any time, though it goes nicely with the egg bag. The magician produces egg after egg from the mouth of an assistant, or a volunteer. The mouth is shown empty, and the egg is removed and placed into a clear bowl or on a tray in full view of everyone. You can produce as many eggs as you wish. And they are real eggs—you can have them broken at any time and demonstrate that fact conclusively.

You can also use Ping-Pong balls, and you can find the objects in your own mouth if you prefer. A very adaptable comic routine to amaze kids or adults.

$1.25

Abracadabra Magic Shop
280 Hamilton St.
Rahway, N.J. 07065

DOUBLE SHOT ROUTINE

An unprepared napkin produces two brimming shot glasses at the same time. Then they vanish. Can be done close-up, away from all chairs and tables. Also works well as part of a stage routine.

$7

The Emporium of Magic
Building A, Suite 110
17220 W. Eight Mile Rd.
Southfield, Mich. 48075

FRAMED

The magician has a magazine with a picture of a beautiful girl on the cover. He also has an empty picture frame. Suddenly the head of the girl from the front cover of the magazine has vanished. The cut-out hole allows you to look in and read the next page. The head reappears inside the picture frame. This is a clever and unexpected trick.

The frame measures 14×10½ inches, and the magazine has a cardboard cover.

$20

Tom Fitzgerald
2814 Washington St.
Wilmington, Del. 19802

I'LL START AGAIN

Paddle effects are very popular for working close to people. The paddle is just what the name implies—a piece of wood shaped like an oar, with a narrow handle.

Here's a good routine for beginners. You draw three chalk lines on the paddle on each side, and the fun begins. The lines disappear. They jump from top to bottom and back again. Every time you say, "I'll start again," they reappear. Finally all the lines are erased and a single line appears, a line running the entire length of the paddle.

$4

Abracadabra Magic Shop
280 Hamilton St.
Rahway, N.J. 07065

FLAMING HEAD CHEST

A beautifully designed and decorated chest is placed over the head, on the shoulders of anyone you choose. A long flaming brass torch is pushed into the cabinet and apparently through your assistant's head as well. When the cabinet is opened at the front, back, and top, the head has vanished. The audience can see through the cabinet to the background behind you. You can wave your hand behind the cabinet, walk behind it, and all around it. They know they are seeing through it—and yet the volunteer cannot really have lost his head.

This chest can be carried under your arm, and yet carries all the impact of much larger equipment. It can be done while surrounded. Flaming torch included.

$75

Aladdin Magic Shop
110 S. High St.
Columbus, Ohio 43215

BALL AND TUBE

You can do it, and they cannot. That's the theme of many popular tricks and stunts that seem even more impossible because the spectator has actually handled the equipment himself without coming up with any solution.

Here is a brass tube and a solid ball. The ball won't fit in the tube—and yet it does for you. You hold it and it slips slowly down inside, then rises up again into view. Others try to do this, but with no success.

$2.50

Abbott's Magic Co.
Colon, Mich. 49040

THIMBLE JUMBO

Your hands are shown empty. Suddenly a thimble appears on the first finger of your hand. You take away the thimble and put it in a pocket—but there it is, back again! This happens again and again, for a total of four thimble productions. Then a final thimble appears—a jumbo, three times as large as any of the others!

You can do this after a little practice, and you can also do a second, entirely different routine. All of the instructions and gimmicks you need are included.

$5

Samuel Berland
517 S. Jefferson St.
Chicago, Ill. 60607

KNIFE THROUGH COAT

A pocket knife is shown, and a spectator's coat is borrowed. The coat is stretched firm by two assisting spectators. Take the knife, open its blade, and thrust the blade right through the cloth of the coat. The blade is actually seen penetrating the cloth. When the blade is removed, close examination fails to reveal any damage to the coat. This can be done without preparation. The original, superior form of this stunt is provided to you by means of full, illustrated directions.

$1

Flosso Hornmann
304 W. 34th St.
New York, N.Y. 10001

LINKING ROPES

Ask spectators to take three lengths of rope and tie them into loops. Take the loops and proceed to link them and unlink them in a baffling manner. To conclude, hand the ropes back to the spectators, who can untie them and see they are ordinary. This is the famous linking-ring effect in an even more amazing form.

climax, toss the balloon into the air, stab at it with the point of the needle, and the balloon bursts with a resounding bang!

Everything you need is included, even extra balloons.

$6.50

Lou Tannen
1540 Broadway
New York, N.Y. 10036

$2.50

Flosso Hornmann
304 W. 34th St.
New York, N.Y. 10001

NO-BURST BALLOON

Blow up a transparent rubber balloon in front of the audience. Then slowly and deliberately push a long needle into one end and out the other. It's real—there is no special gimmick used. The needle is threaded with a length of string that passes right through the balloon. For a rousing

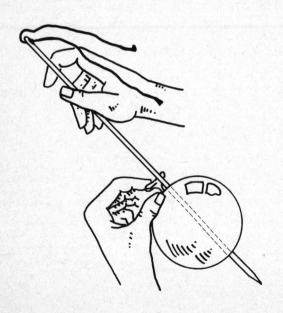

HIPPETY-HOPPETY CHIPS

Make your friends think you are a master sleight-of-hand worker. Show them four aces and place the cards on the table. A poker chip is magically produced and mysteriously passes underneath the cards, appearing first under one, then another. Finally, four poker chips are discovered, one under each ace. The chips are removed, put in your pocket, but when the cards are lifted, there the chips are—under the aces again.

This is a surprisingly easy-to-do close-up routine. Any cards will do.

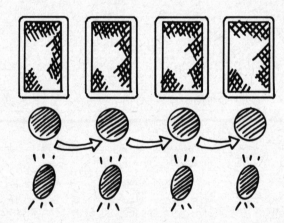

$1

Glenn Comar
353 E. Sixth Ave.
Roselle, N.J. 07203

PULL THROUGH

The magician drapes a silken cord on a solid aluminum bobbin that is skewered by a pencil. The metal bobbin—it looks like a little spool—is about 1½ inches long. Although the spectator is tightly holding the cord, it manages to melt right through the bobbin and the pencil.

This is a truly sensational effect that will last as long as it is safe for people to examine it—forever! No one will ever find out the secret.

$2.50

Lou Tannen
1540 Broadway
New York, N.Y. 10036

THE ENCHANTED RING

Talk about close-up spectaculars! This is one that can be done—well, not just close, because the spectator is actually holding onto the props when the miracle occurs. And everything can be completely examined. It takes just three little items to make a mystery they will never figure out.

The first item is a large hat pin. The second is a metal ring. The third is a 1-inch wooden cube with a hole in it for the pin, and a slot in it for the ring.

You take the ring and fit it into the slot. Then you stick the pin in the hole so that it goes right through the block of wood and right through the inside of the ring, too. The ring is now locked into place.

The spectator sticks out a finger and you hang the ring on the end of it. The pin and cube dangle from the ring and are suspended in midair. The magician puts his hand underneath and lifts his palm so that the block of wood is resting on it. Immediately the block of wood, and the pin, are resting on the magician's palm—and they are completely separate from the ring, which is still held by the spectator.

Everything can now be inspected by the baffled watcher. This one is worth every penny of its price.

$17.50

Lou Tannen
1540 Broadway
New York, N.Y. 10036

IMPROVED DIE TUNNEL

Sometimes the simplest tricks are the most baffling. This is a good case in point. You show a little plastic tube that folds up. You square it up and show that it is empty. Then you show an ordinary die just under 1 inch square. After your friends have examined the die carefully, push it slowly into the tube. When it comes out the other side the number that was on top has been changed to another number.

$3.50

Lou Tannen
1540 Broadway
New York, N.Y. 10036

ROTA DIE

A die is shown sealed in a small plastic box that has a transparent cover. You pass the box to a spectator and ask him or her to shake it to try to turn the die over and change the number that is on top. After spending some time trying to do this, they will decide, quite sensibly, that there is no way they can make the spot change. When they give the box back to you, shake it once and the number has switched.

"Give it back! I want to see that again!" they'll cry. Give the die and box back to them and let them examine it further, but the die will only change for you. This is a real fooler.

$2.50

Lou Tannen
1540 Broadway
New York, N.Y. 10036

RIBBON PENETRATION

One of the most popular forms of magic is one that everybody knows is impossible—making two solid objects pass through each other. Here is an attractive penetration of solid through solid that will leave your audience amazed. It is always ready and it is deceptively simple.

A continuous loop of ribbon is shown to a spectator, who is asked to notice that it has two solid rings threaded on it. With one ring in each hand, the ribbon is passed around the spectator's finger. In a flash the ribbon penetrates right through without injuring the finger.

They believe this possible only because they have seen it themselves. Even that may not be enough to convince them.

$1

Lou Tannen
1540 Broadway
New York, N.Y. 10036

RIBBON FANTASTIQUE

A pocket penetration surprise that looks good and performs even better! This time it is a ribbon that penetrates through a piece of smart-looking, durable plastic. An attractive frame is shown—it looks like a window frame with a crossbar in the middle, but it has no top edge. A piece of clear plastic is inserted into the frame from the top. The plastic has a row of holes across the middle which line up with corresponding holes in the crossbar.

This allows you to take a ribbon and thread it through the holes all the way across, clearly tying the frame and the window together. You give the ends of the ribbon to a pair of spectators. After you give a yank, the plastic slips out, leaving the perfectly solid ribbon behind, still threaded, still with the ends in the hands of the spectators. Another miracle!

$6.50

Lou Tannen
1540 Broadway
New York, N.Y. 10036

BLITZ COCKTAIL

Read this carefully. Every word is true, even though it seems impossible:

You show a large plastic glass that is empty. You can see through it. Show a second glass, also empty. The two are put together, rim to rim, and you make the movements of shaking a cocktail. At first, nothing happens. Then, slowly, the glasses start filling with liquid. As you keep shaking, more and more liquid appears until the glasses are completely filled. The liquid may be milk, water, a soft drink, anything you like, and can be handed out to the audience to taste later.

Can be done for any size audience, onstage, or in the middle of your living room.

$7

Tom Fitzgerald
2814 Washington St.
Wilmington, Del. 19802

MYSTERIOUS BLOCK ESCAPE

Six blocks, each a different color, are in a wooden box. Everything can be examined. The box is closed, though the block colors can still be seen through holes on both sides. A magic wand is put through the holes in the box and the blocks so that it is impossible to remove any of the blocks.

In spite of that, two blocks do escape. They are blocks of the same two colors previously chosen by the audience. A member of the audience can hold the wand, if you desire, and the trick can be immediately repeated. As before, everything can be examined. This is an ideal effect for children's shows, for close-up work, for stage performances, or for shows in your own living room.

$20

Tom Fitzgerald
2814 Washington St.
Wilmington, Del. 19802

CHIP AHOY

A series of surprises involving a poker chip that can be examined at any time. A solid chip is shown, and suddenly a cigarette or pen or pencil is pushed through it, leaving behind a hole. The chip is threaded on a ribbon which penetrates right through so that the chip falls off. Finally, the magician rubs the hole away so that he is again left with a solid poker chip that can be passed for examination. Easy to learn.

$5

Glenn Comar
353 E. Sixth Ave.
Roselle, N.J. 07203

FRESH FISH

Here is an amusing version of the famous torn-and-restored-paper trick. You tell a clever story about a fish store that had a sign reading "Fresh Fish Sold Here Today," which you now hold. Gradually the sign gets destroyed as you tear off one word at a time during the course of the story. The store owner gets very angry until all the pieces of torn paper are magically restored, along with the owner's sense of humor. It is a fun story and a clever trick. You get everything, including enough paper strips to allow you to perform this a dozen times.

$2

Healey's Magic Co.
1612 Dickson Ave.
Scranton, Pa. 18509

STAGING SMALL STAGE ILLUSIONS WITH STYLE

There are many wonderful and classic magic effects that fall somewhere between the magic you casually perform for a few friends in your living room, and the grand act you would do at Madison Square Garden as thousands cheer. In this category you find such things as linking rings (where several seemingly solid steel rings seemingly dissolve into each other), vanishings, levitations, and even larger-scale illusions where it appears that life or limb is in danger. All of these are perfect for working from a stage or in a club. They can be "showy" yet simply done, or they can call for more elaborate measures, but they keep an audience enthralled.

Among the most effective small stage effects are productions. The production of something from the air is probably the most beautiful kind of legerdemain. Cardini did a drunk act that was mostly productions. A slightly tipsy British gentleman kept finding his hands full of cigarettes, then fans of cards, then coins and whatnot. A most "distressing" kind of thing for the performer but amusing to the audience.

Flowers make lovely productions, as do colorful silks. Take a few boards and fold them together and pull out a pile of large objects, spring (pop-up) flowers, and glasses full of liquid—or even bowls of fire. That's the kind of magic that will keep an audience attentive.

Small stage illusions can be extremely impressive, and they range from the very difficult to the very easy. Choose your effects to fit your skills, but keep your audience enthralled with showmanship even if you are doing the easiest effects.

THE BEER CAN ACT

This is not just one trick; it's a whole, complete act! And it's available nowhere else!

Cash in on the beer-can-collecting craze with a beer-can act suitable for presentation to groups of collectors or a young fan's birthday party. This same act can be used for adult or child audiences, since so many young boys and their fathers collect beer cans. Or it makes a nice change-of-pace act for men's groups.

Nothing is more common than a beer can! Imagine being able to vanish, produce, change colors, shrink, etc., with such a common prop. Make your own props according to directions.

Instructions include using beer cans to make things appear and disappear, using them to magically transfer items from one can to another, and using them to make things appear in a borrowed hat. They can change size or brands.

Many other effects are possible. All you need are empty beer cans, instructions, a few common tools, and some ordinary bits and pieces probably in your home right now. Also includes the complete presentation and suggestions for changes and options you might like.

$5

Warner's Magic Factory
Box 455
Hinsdale, Ill. 60521

THE LORING CHECKER MYSTERY

A beautiful cabinet is shown, decorated in Chinese red and gold. It has back and front doors so that you can look right through it. There is also a handsome cover. The doors of the cabinet are closed and opened to reveal the magical appearance of three glasses of water and two large silks. A stack of seven different-colored checkers, each 4 inches in diameter, is put in the box and the door is closed. The cover for the checkers is put in the other side and that door is closed. Presto! They have changed places. The cover is placed over one of the glasses of water and the water appears to change places with the checkers inside the cabinet. This kind of thing keeps up until finally a fourth glass of water is revealed.

The checkers can be shown to be separate at any time, and there is really only room in each side of the cabinet for one glass of water, so it is not at all clear to anyone where the stuff is being produced from. Supply your own silks.

$50

Magic, Inc.
5082 N. Lincoln Ave.
Chicago, Ill. 60625

THE SUCKER DIE BOX

This is a surefire laugh getter, and is ideal for kids or adults. It is easy to do because all the action is done mechanically.

The performer shows a box that contains two compartments, each one just the size of a large die (half a pair of dice). He also shows a hat or paper bag. The die is put into the box, and he says he is going to make it disappear. The two top doors and the two side doors are closed, then the box is tilted sideways and the two doors of the top compartment are opened.

Naturally, the audience is pretty suspicious—especially since they heard the die sliding down to the other side of the box. There is a lot of fun while the performer keeps "sliding" the die from one compartment to another, each time opening only one set of doors. Finally he opens all doors, the die has vanished, and a child is asked to take the die out of the hat or bag, which is where it magically reappears. Easy to do.

$25

Flosso Hornmann
304 W. 34th St.
New York, N.Y. 10001

PROFESSIONAL SQUARE CIRCLE

The square circle is one of the most common methods of making a large quantity of silks, confetti, etc., magically appear. This version is stage-sized with a box 9×11 inches, trimmed in black, white, and gold. Overall height on stand is 16 inches, and the inside tube is 7 inches in diameter. You get everything with this except the items that you produce.

Basically there is a square box with a cut-out

design that allows the spectators to look inside. What they see inside is a cylinder or tube. The magician picks up the box and shows it to the audience, looking through it at them so they can see him through the empty box. Then he puts the box down with the cut-outs in full view, and picks up the cylinder. He shows that it is empty also and looks through it at the audience.

The cylinder goes back into the box, and then, after a magic wave of the hands, out comes an enormous quantity of material—silks, flowers, candles, doves, whatever you have prepared in advance.

$33.50

Healey's Magic Co.
1612 Dickson Ave.
Scranton, Pa. 18509

HAT LOADER

As a magician, you must know how to produce things out of an empty hat. With the hat loader, you can produce a large variety of articles at any time, from a borrowed hat. In working this effect, the magician shows a colorful container, which is filled with confetti. He pours some of the confetti into the hat. Then, waving his wand over the hat, he reaches into the hat and produces a wooden egg, several silks, a large 20-foot garland streamer, and a glass of milk. Nothing is hidden on your body, and you can perform this in centerstage, away from tables.

Make your own hat loader quickly and easily with these instructions. Many other items can be produced as shown.

$1

Warner's Magic Factory
Box 455
Hinsdale, Ill. 60521

THE ULTIMATE HAND CHOPPER

The frame is lacquered wood and the blade unit is heavy and made of metal. Together they make a little guillotine into which a spectator puts his hand. On either side of the hand the magician

puts carrots or celery. The blade is inserted in the top and pushed down. The carrot and celery are cut in two and fall. At the same time the spectator's hand is seen to fall into the receptacle in front.

The magician, who says he has never performed this before, is horror-stricken. He removes the blade, showing only a blank space where the volunteer's hand should be. He reaches into the draped receptacle and picks up the severed hand, which is placed back and magically restored.

Obviously sensational.

$50

Glenn Comar
353 E. Sixth Ave.
Roselle, N.J. 07203

CABINET OF CANTON

A simple wooden tube is shown. Many holes have been drilled through the top and bottom of the tube. A number of solid 6-inch spikes are shown, all mounted onto a wooden frame with a handle.

A balloon is blown up and put in the tube. (The tube is on a stand so the audience can see underneath.) The spikes are lowered and the balloon breaks. The magician is surprised, but puts his arm in anyway and the spikes are seen to protrude from the bottom of the cabinet. The magician attempts to move his arm out, but it is stuck. The spikes are lifted and the arm comes out safely.

$35

Glenn Comar
353 E. Sixth Ave.
Roselle, N.Y. 07203

SANDS OF THE DESERT

This is one of the most beautiful and colorful effects in magic, and is deservedly popular. A large fish bowl is shown and filled with water. This is a clear glass bowl. Three bowls of sand are also shown—each one is a different color.

The performer changes the water to ink, and then places a handful of sand from each bowl into the liquid and mixes thoroughly.

Members of the audience then call out a color of their choice, and as each is called for the performer reaches into the ink and removes only the sand of the requested color. And the sand appears by the handful—completely dry! This is repeated for the two remaining colors. For a finale, the ink is transformed back into water. Then everything can be examined.

Comes complete with fish bowl, six smaller bowls, instructions, and enough sand to cross the desert with—plus everything necessary to change the water to ink and back again.

$30

Healey's Magic Co.
1612 Dickson Ave.
Scranton, Pa. 18509

DELUXE PHANTOM TUBE

A large, handsomely decorated metal tube is shown empty. The tube is 9 inches tall by 4 inches in diameter. To further prove it is empty, you push your wand through it and pour a glass of water through it. Two pieces of ordinary newspaper are shown on both sides and then capped with rubber bands over both ends of the tube. The performer now breaks the paper at one end and starts extracting a large assortment of articles.

$15

Flosso Hornmann
304 W. 34th St.
New York, N.Y. 10001

ORIENTAL RICE BOWLS

Two bowls of rice are shown empty. One is filled to the brim with rice. It is covered with the empty bowl and—magically—the quantity of rice is shown to be doubled. The overflowing rice is leveled off from one bowl and now the rice vanishes and the bowl is filled with water, which is poured from bowl to bowl.

$15

Flosso Hornmann
304 W. 34th St.
New York, N.Y. 10001

FLOWERS FROM FINGERTIPS

Showing his hand empty, the magician reaches into the air and produces a beautiful flower at his fingertips. He throws the flower into a hat, again shows his hand empty, and produces another flower. This can be repeated as many

times as required. At conclusion, the hat is filled with flowers, which the magician can graciously pass out to the ladies in the audience. No skill required, because a clever gimmick does the trick for you.

$1.50

Flosso Hornmann
304 W. 34th St.
New York, N.Y. 10001

DELUXE ZOMBIE

This is an attractive aluminum ball that weighs only 2 ounces, so it is easy to manipulate through the entire routine. The performer takes a piece of cloth and throws it over the ball, which proceeds to float into the air, bob over the edge of the cloth, pop up in the center, peek out the sides, roll along the top edge, vanish, reappear, etc. A stunning one-man effect that includes ball, nifty stand, and directions.

$15

Flosso Hornmann
304 W. 34th St.
New York, N.Y. 10001

HIPPITY-HOP RABBITS

Two attractive cutouts of a white rabbit and a black rabbit are shown. A cover decorated with a white top hat is placed over the white rabbit, and one with a black top hat is placed over the black rabbit. The cutouts then switch places several times, so that the black rabbit appears under the white hat and the white rabbit under the cover with the black hat on it.

This happens several times, but in a very suspicious manner, because the magician always turns the covers around. There is only one obvious explanation—that the black rabbit is white on the reverse side, and the white rabbit is black on its reverse side. The audience is not slow to complain about this obvious trickery, but finally the reverse sides are shown. The white rabbit is red on the back, and the black rabbit is yellow on the reverse side.

This is a clever and comic effect suitable for children's shows. The rabbits are well made and attractively lacquered, and they stand upright on neat black bases.

$19.50

Flosso Hornmann
304 W. 34th St.
New York, N.Y. 10001

LIQUID APPEAR

An empty glass tumbler is shown and visibly dropped into a container. A cover is placed over the container, the magic word is spoken, and the cover is removed. When the glass is taken out it is filled to the top with milk, cola, etc. You then pour the liquid from the glass. Container may be examined. Self-working.

The screen is folded into a triangle and a large number of things appear from the inside, even a rabbit or dove if you want. Each panel is solid and decorated attractively with a Buddha design.

$10

Flosso Hornmann
304 W. 34th St.
New York, N.Y. 10001

$5

Flosso Hornmann
304 W. 34th St.
New York, N.Y. 10001

CANDLE-LITE

You may carry a candle flame from one candle to another, back and forth, or remove the flame from a candle and carry it up to your mouth to light a cigarette, etc. In this method, the flame may be carried visibly if desired. The hands may be shown front and back at any time. Simple to use and good! Exciting to watch, but perfectly safe to perform.

TEMPLE SCREEN

An attractive three-fold screen is shown on the inside, folded flat, then opened out and shown on the outside. Spectators see both sides of the panels, each of which measures 9×12 inches.

$3

Flosso Hornmann
304 W. 34th St.
New York, N.Y. 10001

CANDY FACTORY

A glass overflowing with sugar is shown. You can pour out some of the sugar and let spectators taste it. You then show a fancy metal tube and poke your wand through it to prove it is empty. The tube is placed over the glass. Then the tube is removed and the sugar has vanished and the glass is filled with candy, which may be passed out to the audience.

With this device you can also change a glass of loose tobacco into a glass of cigarettes and make a glass of milk vanish. No skill required.

$10

Flosso Hornmann
304 W. 34th St.
New York, N.Y. 10001

$5

Flosso Hornmann
304 W. 34th St.
New York, N.Y. 10001

CHINESE LINKING RINGS

One of the most popular and mystifying tricks ever presented. A number of nickel-plated rings

COMEDY FUNNEL

This is the perfect prop for the comedy magician. A wonderful trick for children's shows. Place the funnel under the assistant's arm, pump his other arm, and liquid flows out from the funnel. The flow is always under the magician's control, and the funnel can be shown empty and used at any time. This can be combined nicely with the vanishing milk pitcher so that milk can be poured into a kid's ear and funneled out the other side, etc.

are handed out for examination. They are 8 inches in diameter and absolutely solid. The magician then takes these rings and causes them to link and unlink, forming them into all sorts of shapes and figures. Finally all the rings are linked together, but fall apart at the word of command.

$20

Flosso Hornmann
304 W. 34th St.
New York, N.Y. 10001

CHEN LEE WATER SUSPENSION

An open-ended cylinder is passed for examination. It is 3 inches in diameter and 5½ inches high. Then water is poured into it but fails to come out the bottom. A silk is passed through the tube, and comes out dry. Then a glass is pushed up through the tube and emerges at the top—full of water! It's not often that such an unusual effect hits the magic market, and this one is very popular.

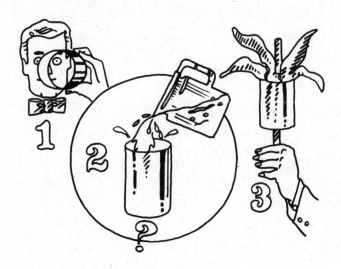

$6

Flosso Hornmann
304 W. 34th St.
New York, N.Y. 10001

HAUNTED RED BARN

The perfect effect for a children's show. First you show a little model of a red barn in the middle of a field. The model is 3-D, and is made of wood lacquered in red, green, and black. The barn is supposed to be haunted, and it does seem to be. First the roof rises open. Every time you close it, it opens again. Then it opens and closes on its own. You get your fingers rapped by it, then your nose is caught.

Next, a ghost appears and sticks to your fingers. It is a white silk handkerchief that seems to do everything except disappear, in spite of all your efforts to get rid of it. There is a lot of excitement when the kids think they have caught you trying to trick them, but they end up twice as baffled in the end. The ghost does disappear finally, appears unexpectedly somewhere else, and chases you offstage. This is funny magic, and exciting. Use any white silks.

$12

Glenn Comar
353 E. Sixth Ave.
Roselle, N.J. 07203

FOUR COKES IN HAND

A silk materializes from thin air, then a full-sized bottle of Coca-Cola appears at the fingertips. Suddenly a second bottle appears, vanishes behind the silk, and reappears. Then the third and fourth bottles appear in quick succession.

The bottles are produced at the fingertips. No table is needed. A little practice will ensure sensational handling of this one. Silk not included.

$9

Glenn Comar
353 E. Sixth Ave.
Roselle, N.J. 07203

COKE COKE COKE

Many full-sized bottles of Coca-Cola are produced from a single unprepared silk.

First a 24-inch silk is displayed or produced. The silk is pulled through your fingers, shown on both sides, etc. Suddenly a bottle of Coca-Cola appears from the silk. As it is being taken away to be put in a crate or on a side table, another appears. When it is taken away a third one shows up, and then another. Up to a dozen bottles can be produced.

This is a beautiful effect, but requires a little practice to produce the indescribable effect. Comes complete with bottles and silk.

$8

Glenn Comar
353 E. Sixth Ave.
Roselle, N.J. 07203

PASS A COCA-COLA

A bottle of Coca-Cola is shown (a real bottle that you supply yourself) and two folding tubes, one red and one yellow. You say you will pass the bottle from one tube to the next, but the audience complains and demands that you do so invisibly, without using your hands. After some more fun that is just what happens. The bottle of Coke is shown to be definitely under the red tube and then the tube is lifted, the bottle is gone and reappears under the yellow tube. At that point the bottle is opened and a glass of the drink is poured out for a member of the audience to enjoy.

The specially designed device that makes the trick work is supplied along with the routine and two neatly made tubes. This requires no special moves, no sleight-of-hand or special training. It is self-working.

$6.50

Glenn Comar
353 E. Sixth Ave.
Roselle, N.J. 07203

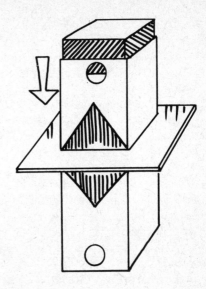

LUCKY LOOPS

A length of rope is shown coiled around the hands. It is in one piece and without knots. The ends are tied together, but magically, three more knots appear tied to the doubled length of rope. They are real knots, but when the magician begins untying one, a whole separate loop of rope drops off. This is repeated for each of the other knots.

The magician unties the final knot on the length of rope he is left holding, tosses the rope in the air, and shows that it too has changed and become a large single loop.

The trick is self-contained and does not require a lot of extra rope to be used as replacements.

$6

Glenn Comar
353 E. Sixth Ave.
Roselle, N.J. 07203

PENTA-BLOCK

Two nicely decorated square wooden tubes are put on top of each other with a piece of plastic in between. The magician takes a brightly lacquered wooden cube that can be examined and drops it into the top tube. It drops out the bottom, and holes in the sides of the tubes allow spectators to watch it go right through.

$18

Glenn Comar
353 E. Sixth Ave.
Roselle, N.J. 07203

THE TARBELL EGG BAG

The egg bag is one of the most popular effects in magic, and is widely used by young performers, or for young audiences. In this case, the bag is of Scotch plaid.

What happens varies from one performer to another, and there are dozens of possible routines. The essence is the mysterious appearance and disappearance of eggs. The bag is empty one minute, and full of eggs the next minute. With this model you can even have the spectator reach in and remove the egg from the bag. Don't worry—he'll never discover a thing.

Along with this ingeniously constructed bag comes an equally clever and entertaining routine used by Dr. Harlan Tarbell, one of the great names in magic. Also included are step-by-step instructions and a wooden egg.

$4

Lou Tannen
1540 Broadway
New York, N.Y. 10036

DELUXE CLOCK VANISH

The clock has a shiny chrome outside and a printed face, and there is celluloid over the face. It looks like a real clock even up close.

You pick up the clock and show it all around and bang it on the table to show that it is really solid. Then put it on a thin plaque, which you wave in the air before announcing, "The clock is gone."

No one will believe you, and they'll insist it is still hiding behind the plaque. You let the uproar build for a while and then turn the plaque around to show that the clock really is gone. In fact, the plaque has a statement on it that reads, "My, how time flies!"

This is a fun miniature illusion that can be used in a great many ways. For example, the clock can be vanished under a cloth or inside a newspaper, or in just about any other way you can think of. Or you can change it to flowers or candy.

The effect is entirely self-contained, so it can be worked away from all tables and chairs.

$6

Lou Tannen
1540 Broadway
New York, N.Y. 10036

BALANCE IMPOSSIBLE

Superman could leap tall buildings with a single bound, but he could not just leap into the air and stay there in one spot. Now you can show some equipment that does what Superman couldn't.

You take a clear round plastic rod that is ½ inch in diameter, and two ordinary clear water glasses. The rod is held parallel with the ground and the two glasses are turned upside down and balanced side by side.

Normally anyone would think that was pretty terrific, but then you turn the stick upside down and the two glasses just hang there in midair, touching nothing but the breeze and the polished rod. To emphasize the fact that the laws of nature are being defied, you can pour a soft drink or any other liquid into the glasses while they remain suspended.

When finished, the glasses can be handed out to be inspected. There is nothing to conceal, and no skill is necessary. You will be able to do this immediately upon receipt.

$4.50

Lou Tannen
1540 Broadway
New York, N.Y. 10036

ALUMINUM CHINK-A-CHINK

This is a whole routine that can be solemn or funny, depending on your needs at the moment. A series of carefully machined cups made of solid aluminum appear and disappear under your hands until they have all traveled around and have ended up—mysteriously!—all together under the same hand. A little practice is required, but all of the difficult sleight-of-hand moves you might expect have been eliminated.

$12.50

Lou Tannen
1540 Broadway
New York, N.Y. 10036

SPONGE BALLS

This is a standard item in the repertoire of most magicians. An endless combination of appearances and vanishes and transformations are possible with these colorful little balls. They are spongy and compress to very little space in your fingers, yet can do a host of astonishing things. In fact, the sponge balls offered here are machine-made and perfectly round. Each set comes in a choice of colors—natural, yellow, or red.

The routine that comes with these is said to be the easiest method of making the little balls baffle the audience. They vanish from your hands and appear in a spectator's hand. They vanish and appear, and they multiply so that one turns into two and then three and then four. And that's only the beginning. A handful of sponge balls is like a deck of cards—the possibilities are endless.

Try some. If you get intrigued, there are whole books written on the subject. You'll be amazed at the range of possibilities.

Four 1-inch balls $1.50
Four 2-inch balls $2.50
Four 3-inch balls $4

Lou Tannen
1540 Broadway
New York, N.Y. 10036

SPONGE BALL TO RABBIT

Here is a cute addition to any sponge-ball routine. The magician places a 1½-inch sponge ball in his closed left hand and apparently sneaks it away with his right hand. The spectator is asked to guess which hand the ball is really in. Surprise! The ball has vanished, and when the hands are opened what you show instead is a cute little rabbit with two eyes, ears, and everything. He is about 3 inches high. This works alone or can be added to any other sponge-ball trick or routine.

$4.50

Lou Tannen
1540 Broadway
New York, N.Y. 10036

THE TIGHTROPE BALL

This is the story of the tightrope ball, which sits on a little stand during the act. It is the story of some treasures that came in a box that was a gift from Satan! A length of silk rope is displayed, and before long the rope is stretched out between both hands and touched to the ball. Immediately the ball sits on the rope. You lift it away from the stand, and when you order it to, it begins to roll along the rope from side to side.

No, it isn't really a demon inside that makes the ball move, but something a lot safer to deal with than that. Children will love this, and so will you. Comes complete with an amusing story for you to tell as the ball goes through its paces.

$3

Lou Tannen
1540 Broadway
New York, N.Y. 10036

CHEFLAO BOX

This is a production box with a real difference. It has four sides all right, but no top and no bottom. How could anything be hidden inside? You show the four sides separately and put them together by means of interlocking slots and holes—very simple. Then you reach inside and pull out any number of silks, ribbons, flowers, etc.

This is a quality product that will last a lifetime.

$50

Tom Fitzgerald
2814 Washington St.
Wilmington, Del. 19802

BACKSTAGE

This is not only a good mystery, it is a fine comedy effect. The magician has a cloth-covered tray. On the tray are two boards. He stands with his back to the audience so they can see what "really" happens. A large playing card is put between two boards, but the audience can see that he has dropped the card between two ribbons. Now the trick is repeated, but this time the audience will see the effect from the front.

The card disappears between the two boards, and the magician again shows that the card is in the ribbons. The boards are put away empty, but when the cloth that covers the tray is removed, the card really has disappeared.

$25

Tom Fitzgerald
2814 Washington St.
Wilmington, Del. 19802

DISAPPEARING BOTTLES

The effect of this is simple and direct, like that of all truly great magic. Some bottles are placed in a paper bag. The bag is crushed and the bottles have vanished. This comes complete with metal bottles—not fake ones of paper or rubber. This works by an entirely different principle from the usual method, and does not require a special table.

$40

Tom Fitzgerald
2814 Washington St.
Wilmington, Del. 19802

GERMAN SEALED MILK GLASS

This mechanical gem consists of a 12-ounce clear-plastic tumbler that has imitation milk sealed inside. It never has to be emptied or filled. Toss it in your suitcase and it is ready to go.

You can apparently pour milk from the glass into anything, such as a paper cone, a person's pocket, a girl's purse, a boy's ear—and then show that the milk has gone from the glass, leaving only a small quantity in the bottom. Of course no milk ever really leaves the glass—it just seems to.

$8.50

Aladdin Magic Shop
110 S. High St.
Columbus, Ohio 43215

THE FLASH DIE

A large die materializes at your fingertips in full view of the audience, with a brilliant flash of light! This may be done in connection with the sliding die box, for stage work, or close-up. It is visual magic that you will love, and that will leave the audience amazed.

$17.50

John Cornelius
430 Elmwood
San Antonio, Tex. 78212

HAND CREMATION

This is a completely unusual and unexpected little illusion that can be done to perfection even at close range while being carefully watched from all sides.

A small open chest is locked onto a spectator's wrist. His hand fills the chest. A tube is slid down over the hand. Liquid is apparently poured onto the hand, and a lit match is dropped in. Flames leap forth and the hand is supposedly consumed. The tube may be removed to show that the hand is gone. Then the hand is restored and the apparatus removed from the spectator's unharmed wrist.

$32

Aladdin Magic Shop
110 S. High St.
Columbus, Ohio 43215

JUMBO CHAIN WELDING

A chest, open front and back, is displayed. The front is closed and an aluminum rod is pushed through the holes in the sides of the chest, so that the rod extends from each side. The ends of the rod are in view at all times.

Ten large 8-inch rings of steel are shown separate and then placed in the chest. Suddenly the rod is lifted up out of the chest and the rings are now on the center of it. The front of the chest is opened and the chest is shown empty.

But that's not all! The rings are slid off the rod into the empty hand, then tossed high into the air. While in midair they become linked together in a long 30-inch chain. This is a real attention-getter.

$40

Aladdin Magic Shop
110 S. High St.
Columbus, Ohio 43215

THE DEVIL'S CANISTER

The Devil's canister is just what you have been looking for if you work without an assistant.

This enables you to gain possession of borrowed rings, bills, secret messages or questions, and so on. You can then reproduce them in any way of your choice.

Here's how it works. You have someone take out a dollar bill and note the serial number. You take out a match and drop it into the canister. Real flames shoot up, filling the whole interior. The spectator drops the bill into the fire, where it is consumed in flames. You remove a sealed envelope from your pocket, tear it open, and remove the spectator's original bill. He proceeds to verify the serial number.

This is wonderful for mindreading. A spectator can write a question on a piece of paper and drop it into the flames. Immediately, and with no stalling, you can answer the question. In the same manner they can drop in their own rings, coins, etc., and you have immediate possession of them to reproduce them a moment later from the air or in any other way you like.

Comes with a manuscript of twenty different uses.

$7.50

Aladdin Magic Shop
110 S. High St.
Columbus, Ohio 43215

TOPIT

Anything you can hold in your hand you can vanish immediately. This device can be used under close-up conditions to exchange objects or to vanish—well, most anything. One magician even used it to vanish a kitten. Complete handbook included.

$3

Magic, Inc.
5082 N. Lincoln Ave.
Chicago, Ill. 60625

FLOATING GLASS

Whether you are just starting to do magic or have been at it long enough to have a wide reputation, this is an effect that will delight you. A glass of milk clings to your fingertips at first, and refuses to fall. Then it actually floats in midair.

No threads or wires are involved, and yet you have complete control over the glass. Routines included.

$3.95

D. Robbins & Co.
127 W. 17th St.
New York, N.Y. 10011

MAGICIAN'S DREAM PRODUCTION

For years magicians have dreamed of producing a large bowl of water (with or without goldfish swimming around) without using chairs or screens, or tables with a large cloth covering them, or some other suspicious sort of hiding place.

Now there is a method! A flower basket with an open screen front is used so that people can see into it at all times. The magician shows a large cloth and shakes it over the basket. When it is whipped away the basket is seen to be full of colored flowers. Then the cloth is draped over his curved arm and the magician, standing away from everything else onstage, reaches under and brings out a large bowl overflowing with flowers. Then another! And only then does he produce a third bowl with two doves in it or else full of water.

The basket is 8×10×6½ inches high. Each bowl is solid, 9 inches in diameter and 4 inches high. This comes complete with bowls, basket, flowers, and cloth. The cloth is innocent and ungimmicked—the basket is what does the trick. This is not only big and spectacular, it is easy to carry.

$42

Aladdin Magic Shop
110 S. High St.
Columbus, Ohio 43215

MOXAHALLA

This is a beautiful routine that makes a good follow-up to the rice bowls, described elsewhere, or an effect that will stand on its own.

A cylinder is shown to be empty from both ends, then it is placed on a tray. A can with water in it is picked up, and water is poured into the cylinder. When the cylinder is lifted, rice pours out instead of water. The cylinder is then allowed to slide down the arm, leaving a glass of milk in the hand. The milk is splashed to show it is real, and then wrapped in paper. A hole is punched in the paper, and when the liquid is poured out it has changed back to water.

The can and cylinder are all that are supplied with this.

$15

Aladdin Magic Shop
110 S. High St.
Columbus, Ohio 43215

GRANT'S POTATO BOX

A chest is opened and seen to contain a potato and a length of ribbon. The potato is passed around to anyone who has not seen a potato before, and while it is being examined the ribbon is threaded through the chest with the ends left sticking out of either end. A ring is borrowed and vanished.

At this point the chest is opened and the potato is taken out. The ribbon is running through the potato. While spectators hold the ends of the ribbon, the potato is sliced in half and there in the center, threaded on the ribbon, is the borrowed ring. This is completely baffling, and many other effects are possible also.

The chest is about 8×5×6 inches.

$22

Aladdin Magic Shop
110 S. High St.
Columbus, Ohio 43215

THE PROFESSOR'S NIGHTMARE

Show three separate pieces of rope, each a different length. These are "stretched" so that they are all the same length. Then each rope is taken separately and shown to be a different length from the others.

Any rope can be used, but one is supplied to start you off. It will need replacing eventually. A story about the professor is also included so you can tell the tale and show the ropes at the same time. Clever and funny.

$1.50

Magic, Inc.
5082 N. Lincoln Ave.
Chicago, Ill. 60625

WONDEROPE

The most famous magic trick in the world is one that careful investigation has proved did not ever exist—the rising rope trick in India. And yet you can do a version of it right now.

A rope is uncoiled any time during your show and rises 8 feet into the air. You can cause it to rise or descend at your will, or remain suspended 3 feet away while you walk around it. No assistants are required, and the rope goes higher than your hands without touching you in any way.

$5

Abbott's Magic Co.
Colon, Mich. 49040

LUNA TRICK

This one is for children, and is a great effect to get them riled up. The "Man in the Moon" used is a large wooden disc with a face painted on it. He is taken from his home, which looks like a cloud, and is placed in a second box that has two doors side by side.

The idea, says the magician, is to "pass" the Man in the Moon magically from the box back to his former home in the clouds. So he tips the box to one side, opens the door that is raised up, and look—no Moon Man. Well, everyone heard the Man in the Moon go "thud" when it rolled down to the other end of the box, so that won't do at all. They want to see the *other* door open.

OK. The magician is perfectly willing to please them. He tilts the box back the other direction and opens what used to be the lower door, which is now up in the air. See, kids, no Man in the

Moon. Now they are really excited because they heard it go "thud" again when it rolled back down the other direction.

That is kept up for a while until finally the magician figures out that they want both doors open at once. Of course the Moon Man is gone, but it turns out he is not back at home in the cloud box either. Oops! As the magician begins to alibi himself, the Man in the Moon peeps over the top of the cloud, which the performer is holding. They all shout for him to look, but every time he turns his head the Moon Man drops back out of sight. This is a guaranteed crowd pleaser for the younger set.

$30

The Emporium of Magic
Building A, Suite 110
17220 W. Eight Mile Rd.
Southfield, Mich. 48075

BLACK HAND GAG

Invite a boy to come up onstage to help you, and start to hand him something. Then lay it down and look around for a towel. Show it carelessly on both sides, then wipe off his hands with it. Shake it out and it is covered with big, black dirty hand marks. Good comedy, and even the victim will be amused.

$2.50

Magic, Inc.
5082 N. Lincoln Ave.
Chicago, Ill. 60625

THE BLOCKBUSTER

Flowers make good openings for an act, and few productions are as sudden or as rousing as this one. Get them to sit up and take notice right away.

A handkerchief is shown empty and draped over the left hand. A lit cigarette is pushed into the handkerchief, a shot is heard, and suddenly colored streamers shoot in the air, followed by the colorful production of a bouquet of spring (pop-up) flowers.

Everything needed is supplied—handkerchief, poppers, bouquet, etc.

$10

The Emporium of Magic
Building A, Suite 110
17220 W. Eight Mile Rd.
Southfield, Mich. 48075

IMPROVED FLOWER IN BUTTONHOLE

The magician remarks that he will show how easy it is to grow a flower by the aid of magic. He places the magic seed on his coat lapel, makes a pass with his wand, and "like a flash" a beautiful flower appears in his buttonhole. No skill is required, and no preparation. It's all in the wand, which is chrome-plated and can be used throughout the show.

$15

Abbott's Magic Co.
Colon, Mich. 49040

50-STAR MISMADE FLAG

The performer rolls a piece of paper into a tube and stuffs three silks inside—a red one, a white one, and a blue one. Only he doesn't seem to notice that he has "accidentally" dropped the blue silk onto the floor, and when the tube is unpacked to reveal a flag, there is only red and white—the blue is missing. The performer smarts under the laughter of the audience and refuses to be defeated. He picks up the mismade flag and the blue silk, puts them in the tube, and finally produces the 50-star flag with the blue in its proper place. This is good comedy that stirs the audience up and is unexpected, too. You can use your own dye tube.

$25

Dye tube $7.50

Rice's Silk King Studio
640 Evening Star Ln.
Cincinnati, Ohio 45220

PRODUCTION ITEMS

Once you have a folding screen or square circle or some other device that lets you produce a large quantity of things, what things will they be? Preferably something that will look big and solid, or at least big and colorful, and which nonetheless folds into a little tiny area so that you can produce items that seem to amount to twenty or thirty times the amount of space you had available—even if the space were filled, which the audience is convinced it wasn't.

Here are some typical items that will get a laugh or two and which are made of foam rubber, painted in lifelike colors. They collapse very small and spring instantly to full size and shape when they are released.

Large red apple $1.50
Yellow banana $1.25
Large carrot $1.75
Brown doughnut $1.25
Small red tomato $1.25
Fish—a large, colorful trout $3.00
Hot dog on a bun $1.75
String of five hot dogs $3.50
Slice of watermelon $1.75
Hamburger $1.75

James Rainho Products
14 Windsor Rd.
Medford, Mass. 02155

COFFEE VASE

This is better than the standard production of a glass of water or milk because unlike the usual effects, this one ends up with a cup of steaming coffee.

A chrome-plated vase and a chromed metal cover are shown. The vase is filled with cotton wool and the cover is placed on top as a heat control as the coffee is brewing. The cover is removed, which leaves the cotton in full view, sticking up over the top. There is a little shallow lid that is put on and taken off, and then the magician pours out steaming coffee.

The metal vase is 9 inches tall and can also be used for the production of silks.

$40

Abbott's Magic Co.
Colon, Mich. 49040

TIPSY BAG

This starts out as if you were going to do an egg-bag routine. Then the drinks start coming. You reach in and produce a cordial for your assistant from the audience, then several shots for yourself, then a glass of beer. Of course, the bag is officially "empty."

$30

Samuel Berland
517 S. Jefferson St.
Chicago, Ill. 60607

TIPSY-TURVY BOTTLES

Two bottles and two cylinders are shown. The spectator is told by the magician, "Do as I do." Each places a cover over the bottle. Each bottle and cover are given a half-turn. When the covers are removed, the magician's bottle is right side up and the volunteer's bottle is upside down. It is repeated with the same results.

$45

Abbott's Magic Co.
Colon, Mich. 49040

FLOATING ELECTRIC LIGHT BULB

This is a fine stage effect that is very puzzling. In appearance, you show an ordinary light bulb or remove one from a lamp. You pass your hand over it and it lights. Then it remains suspended in air, has a hoop passed over it, floats about, moves from place to place, and obeys your commands.

$10

Magic Inc.
5082 N. Lincoln Ave.
Chicago, Ill. 60625

VANISHING BIRD CAGE

The magician shows a bird cage on his outstretched hand. It is all metal and looks solid.

Inside is a canary. Everyone looks closely and the cage vanishes. It is not covered with a cloth or concealed in any way—it simply isn't there any more.

Harry Blackstone has a group come up from the audience and place their hands on every available bit of cage so that it is covered entirely with outstretched hands—and it still vanishes in a trice!

What you get is an all-metal cage and an all-rubber (but lifelike) canary. And everything else that is needed to produce this miracle, including detailed instructions for easy working.

$13.50

Magic, Inc.
5082 N. Lincoln Ave.
Chicago, Ill. 60625

DELUXE MAGIC TEA KETTLE

A beautiful tea kettle of anodized copper is shown and fifteen to twenty glasses are poured from it, the drinks being of various different colors. (The kettle's capacity is 2 quarts.) Where do all these pretty drinks come from? The magician will show you. He takes off the lid and produces so many brightly colored silks (not supplied) that they would overflow the kettle if returned to it.

Now the colored drinks are poured back inside and mixed together. Clear water—or milk, or beer, or whatever—is poured out next. These can be handed to the audience. Two excellent routines are included.

$10

Magic, Inc.
5082 N. Lincoln Ave.
Chicago, Ill. 60625

THE ACROBATIC CANE

You show an attractive black cane with a white tip and cap. You turn it upside down and hold the wrong end. Suddenly the stick leaves your hand and on its own accord turns completely over in the air until the knob end returns to your fingers. It can also cling to your fingers without

any visible support, and can be turned into a complete pantomime stunt.

$10

Magic, Inc.
5082 N. Lincoln Ave.
Chicago, Ill, 60625

PEERLESS BLOCK MYSTERY

This is more than a trick, it is a whole routine.

Three different-colored blocks are shown to be separate from each other, and all solid. Two are stacked on a glass plate, and an empty cover is put over them. The third block is wrapped in a handkerchief—and promptly vanishes. The full shape of the block is seen inside the handkerchief right up to the moment the hanky is empty. The cover is raised and the missing block is seen between the other two.

A hat is borrowed and shown empty. The center block is again vanished from a handkerchief and this time it is found in the hat.

The three blocks are stacked again, the cover is slipped over them, and when it comes up they have changed places.

The cover and the borrowed hat are again shown empty. The three blocks are placed inside the cover, and when it is raised, the middle block has vanished. The cover is shown empty. The missing block is found in the hat.

The blocks are 3-inch cubes. Everything is supplied, including a snappy line of running commentary, but you have to borrow the hat yourself.

$22.50

Magic, Inc.
5082 N. Lincoln Ave.
Chicago, Ill. 60625

TRICKY SHAKER

A clear plastic shaker with a chrome cover is shown and placed in a paper bag. The cover is removed and milk is poured into the shaker. Suddenly you crush the paper bag and toss it to the audience. The shaker and milk have vanished.

This requires the use of a magic milk pitcher, described elsewhere in this catalogue. The shaker itself collapses into the cover when the shaker is placed in the bag.

$5

House of Enchantment
Lake Rd., R.D. 5
Somerset, Pa. 15501

APPEARING ORANGE BOX

A half-dollar is borrowed, marked, and vanished. A chest about 7×12 inches is shown empty. An orange is tied in a bag and placed in the chest. Then the top of the bag is stuck through a hole in the cover of the chest.

In fact, the rest of the bag is pulled through the holes, too. The orange has vanished. The chest is shown empty again. Then the lid is closed and several oranges are produced. These are tossed to the audience. Someone tosses an orange back, and inside is found the missing half-dollar.

$20

House of Enchantment
Lake Rd., R.D. 5
Somerset, Pa. 15501

CRYSTAL FIRE BOWL

The magician enters, shows a heavy cloth on both sides, tosses it over his shoulder, and from under it pulls out a clear crystal bowl of fire! To say the least, this is a startling effect.

No batteries, no cigarette-lighter units.

$5

House of Enchantment
Lake Rd, R.D. 5
Somerset, Pa. 15501

MULTIPLYING CANDLES

The magician plucks a candle from the air, then it turns into two candles, then three. Finally there are four candles in the magician's hands. No skill is required; it works automatically.

$25

Chu's Magic Studio
401 Chatham Rd.
T.S.T.
P.O. Box 5221
Kowloon, Hong Kong

COMEDY EGG TRICK

This is a good stunt for children. An egg is broken into a canister and a card is clamped over the top of the can. The can is then turned upside down and put on top of a boy's head.

The performer pretends to forget what happens next and then remembers that the instructions for the trick are printed on the card under the can. So he pulls out the card and reads it aloud. The instructions are clear, but cause a lot of worrying—"Do not remove this card."

Oops. The magician is worried now, but so is the volunteer, who is busy picturing the egg sitting in undraped splendor on his unprotected hair. All of the audience is picturing the same thing, but the performer has an idea. He gives the boy an egg beater to beat the egg as it falls down because the can is about to be removed. When the can comes away the egg has vanished, much to the volunteer's relief.

The can is now placed on the performer's hand, lifted off, and standing on his hand is a tall glass of candy, which may be passed to the audience or given to the boy who has been helping.

Comes with canister, card, and glass.

$6.25

Aladdin Magic Shop
110 S. High St.
Columbus, Ohio 43215

DOUBLE-LOAD PAGODAS

This is a box with an open front that can change anything into anything else. Change a rabbit to a guinea pig or a dove to silks. Any kind of change you want can be brought about.

Here's one possible effect. You show the cabinet empty and then place a glass of milk inside. When the front is opened, instead of milk the pagoda is full of Ping-Pong balls that scatter all over the audience.

Large (12×8×8 inches) $32.50
Small (10×6×6 inches) $27.50

Aladdin Magic Shop
110 S. High St.
Columbus, Ohio 43215

BROCK'S BLOCK

This is similar to the visible vampire but with some added astonishment. It is a large, heavily built, and beautifully decorated piece of equipment.

The block is suspended from a chain and placed inside a cabinet, from which it can be seen at all times. Two solid plaques are stuck through the cabinet and it not only visibly penetrates them, it also frees itself from a sword that runs through the block and through the cabinet walls.

$52.50

Aladdin Magic Shop
110 S. High St.
Columbus, Ohio 43215

DAGGER CHEST ILLUSION

The head of a girl is encased in a beautifully decorated box. The front is closed and a series of gleaming swords are forced through the sides and top one by one. As soon as all seventeen swords are pushed in, the front is open and the head of the girl is gone.

All that is visible in the box are swords. When the front is closed again, all the swords are removed and the box is reopened to show the head of the girl once more in its proper place.

The dagger chest is well made and packs flat. Can be done anywhere. Comes with a stand for the chest.

$120

Tom Fitzgerald
2814 Washington St.
Wilmington, Del. 19802

VANISHING RADIO

The magician's assistant has a big radio on a tray. The magician covers it with a silk, takes it off the tray, and then carries it forward toward the audience and tosses the silk in the air. The radio is gone!

This is a large console-model radio almost 2 cubic feet in size. Up to now the vanishing radio was never perfect, but this construction is ideal, and allows the effect to be performed anywhere. The tray, on which the radio was standing, can be shown from both sides after the disappearance.

$175

Tom Fitzgerald
2814 Washington St.
Wilmington, Del. 19802

SUITCASE TO TABLE

This is a beautiful magic prop that will not only wow the crowd but will also be a help to you.

The magician enters with a suitcase, and in the space of a single second by the clock it is transformed into a beautiful and sturdy table. As a suitcase, it can hold your entire act. As a table, there is room for all your apparatus. The case size is 23½×9×18 inches and the table's dimensions are 35½×23½×15½ inches.

$100

Tom Fitzgerald
2814 Washington St.
Wilmington, Del. 19802

DIABLO BOTTLE

On the table are a large bottle and four glasses. The magician pours from the bottle into the first glass, and it is a colorless liquid—water. When the glass is filled he takes a white silk from the bottle, and it is completely dry. A second glass is filled, but this time what comes out of the bottle is a red liquid. When the magician has finished pouring, he plucks out a red silk from inside the bottle. It, too, is dry.

The third glass is filled with a green liquid and a green silk is taken from the bottle. The fourth glass is filled with a yellow liquid and a yellow silk appears from the bottle. Now the magician wraps it in a sheet of newspaper, says the magic formula, and breaks the bottle through the middle. He pulls out a big bouquet of feather flowers in beautiful colors.

This is one trick that turns into a whole act all by itself, and you can perform it easily. You must supply the feather flowers yourself, but everything else is included, even the colored liquids.

$40

Tom Fitzgerald
2814 Washington St.
Wilmington, Del. 19802

GRANT'S FLYING FISH

This is something that is baffling beyond words, and a very pretty effect that can be performed close-up and surrounded.

You have two tall glasses, each on a thin wooden coaster. You also show two metal cylinders. The cylinders are empty—the glasses are full of water.

Down goes the cylinder to cover the glass on the left, and a live goldfish appears inside when the cylinder is lifted. The fish is actually in the water—there are no mirrors. Then the fish passes from glass to glass as many times as you wish. Finally the fish vanishes from both glasses and again the covers are empty.

Everything can be examined even though the trickery is built right into the equipment itself. Really wonderful.

$22.50

Lou Tannen
1540 Broadway
New York, N.Y. 10036

HARLEQUIN CIGARETTE HOLDER

If you use a cigarette in your act, then this piece of equipment should definitely be part of your show. It is an entire routine in itself. You start to place a cigarette in a holder when suddenly another cigarette appears there. Not needing two cigarettes, you place one back in your pocket—whereupon the cigarette in the holder vanishes!

Looking slightly annoyed, you again remove the cigarette from your pocket and start to put it in the holder. Again the other cigarette appears there. This is continued until the audience is roaring at your predicament.

You can vanish a cigarette at your fingertips and have it appear in the holder. A cigarette shoved in the ear emerges from the holder, etc. The cigarette may be lit or unlit.

$4.50

Lou Tannen
1540 Broadway
New York, N.Y. 10036

CIGET

This is an electric, self-lighting cigarette dropper. It holds ten cigarettes at a time and gives you the freedom and certainty of performance that make for your peace of mind and a mind-blown audience.

This device is worn under the coat, and by pressure of the fingers, a single cigarette is instantly lighted and dropped into your hand at any time during the act.

$27.50

Lou Tannen
1540 Broadway
New York, N.Y. 10036

CRYSTAL FLOWER TUBE

One of the prettiest, flashiest, most visual tricks in magic—the production of a large number (up to fifty) colored spring flowers from a crystal-clear Lucite tube. The tube is freely displayed, capped at each end with pieces of paper held in place by two fancy bands. The capped tube is shown at both ends, and yet suddenly the tube is filled with flowers. You can break the paper ends and have the flowers shower out into a container. You supply the flowers.

$28.50

Lou Tannen
1540 Broadway
New York, N.Y. 10036

DART FLOWERS

Dart flowers are the ideal kind to have for magical appearances because they come with a pointed base. When these are pulled from a box or hat they can be tossed into the air in such a way that the pointed base will stick in the floor and make a showy display.

Large bouquets and dart flowers of any color are made to order. These come in different sizes and combinations. Ask for specific details.

Twelve-flower bouquet $69.50

Lou Tannen
1540 Broadway
New York, N.Y. 10036

FEATHER FLOWER BOUQUETS

These flowers are mounted on top-grade spring steel, and the feathers pack tightly. These are gorgeous colored flowers that compress into a very small space and open instantly to form extra-large bouquets.

Six-flower regular bouquet $12.95

Lou Tannen
1540 Broadway
New York, N.Y. 10036

MUMMY ASRAH

Here is a miniature version of one of the most famous forms of floating a person. In this case you levitate not a live body, but a dead one—a foot-long wooden mummy.

The mummy is placed on a thin bench that stands several inches above your table, and it is covered with a fancy cloth. You wave your arms over it and it floats up off the bench, still beneath its cloth cover, then away from the bench, and over to one side of the table, almost down to the floor, and up to the fingertips.

At that point you grab a corner of the cloth and toss it into the air. The mummy has vanished completely! The thin bench can be picked up and shown underneath and all around.

This can be worked under almost any conditions. No assistant is necessary. Comes complete.

$15

Lou Tannen
1540 Broadway
New York, N.Y. 10036

THE HEADLESS SPECTATOR

An eager spectator is lured up to the platform and a tube is placed over his head. A square chimney with a glass front is placed over the tube and then lifted to show the spectator's head still visible. Suddenly, the magician changes the spectator's head to a large cabbage, which is removed.

Naturally, once the cabbage is taken away there is nothing in the box. The spectator's head has vanished. Can be done anywhere. Supply your own cabbage, and entice your own spectator.

$60

Lou Tannen
1540 Broadway
New York, N.Y. 10036

TORCH THROUGH ARM

Here's what you've been looking for to liven up your act. You invite a spectator to come up and put his arm into a fancy leatherlike cylinder that you display. Then a large brass torch—with abundant flames—is pushed right through the cylinder and out the other side. Totally apart from your cylinder being in the way of the torch, so is the volunteer's arm.

The torch may be examined after it is removed, and the spectator's arm may also be examined without anyone being any the wiser. Fire magic is always attractive and riveting. This is an effect that ought to be a big success.

$17.50

Lou Tannen
1540 Broadway
New York, N.Y. 10036

DISAPPEARING KNOT

At last a visible vanishing-knot effect that can be done anywhere, anytime, and completely surrounded. Yes! Let them breathe down your rope!

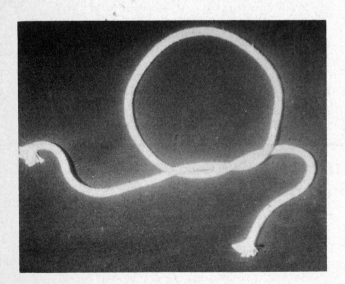

A 42-inch piece of magician's rope, which can be used to do your favorite rope flourishes or tricks, is brought out. You tie a knot in the middle of the rope and let it dangle before the spectator's eyes. Toss rope from hand to hand and make the knot vanish in midair, or simply blow

on it anytime you want. Can be repeated over and over. If you wish, spectator may hold one end of rope in his own hands. Knot can be made to vanish while spectator remains holding end of rope.

Nothing to worry about. No wires, thread-hairs, etc. Completely automatic, self-working.

$3

Guaranteed Magic
27 Bright Rd.
Hatboro, Pa. 19040

ONE TWO ONE ROPE

Two pieces of rope are shown and visibly join into one length of rope that may be tugged on and pulled.

No cutting. Use the same ropes over and over again. No snaps, magnets, cements, no short pieces, no hollow rope!

Here is a great trick which you will use at once, and continue to use in all types of shows. No replacements needed.

$2

Jack Miller Enterprises
119 Weymouth Rd.
Syracuse, N.Y. 13205

SPACE-AGE ROPES

An easy-to-carry effect which can be performed stage or close-up.

The performer shows three equal-length pieces of rope. Each of the ends of the ropes is bound with tape, making it clear that there indeed are three separate pieces. The ends are brought up into the hand, where the three ropes suddenly blend into but one long piece, with only two taped ends.

The startling transformation of the three ropes into one and the vanish of the four taped ends creates a very visual and baffling illusion!

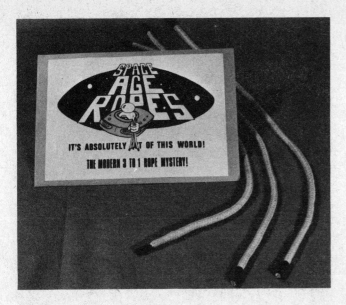

$7.50

Micky Hades International
Box 2242
Seattle, Wash. 98111

FIRE BOWL

The magician shows both sides of a large cloth, throws it over his shoulder, and produces from under it a gleaming bowl of fire. The bowl is of polished stainless steel, and lights electrically at the push of a button. This model is thin and lightweight. Cloth bag included, but no batteries. Use any cloth. Not sold to minors.

$18.50

Theater Effects, Inc.
P.O. Box 293
South Bound Brook, N.J. 08880

POP-UP CANDLE

Wouldn't you like to be able to reach into the air during your performance and produce a gleaming lit candle? This candle springs up and lights automatically, a full 5 inches tall. It is battery-operated and self-working. Twelve lighting elements are included with each candle. Not sold to minors.

$20
Extra lighting elements, per dozen $2.50

Theater Effects, Inc.
P.O. Box 293
South Bound Brook, N.J. 08880

DRAGON WAND

This wand will shoot a streak of fire or a stream of water, whichever you prefer. The water can be squirted out into the audience, or the cane can be filled with powder for a spectacular fire effect. Not sold to minors.

$12.50

Extra powder $2

Theater Effects, Inc.
P.O. Box 293
South Bound Brook, N.J. 08880

CONFETTI LAUNCHER

Here is a new electronic device that makes a large shower of confetti or releases a big ball of fire at any point in your act. It makes a sensational opening, or can serve to distract people from anything. Just step into this shower and make your production. Everyone will be so stunned you can get away with anything. Not sold to minors.

$24.50

Theater Effects, Inc.
P.O. Box 293
South Bound Brook, N.J. 08880

HAND FLASHER

This is a small hand-held and hand-operated flashpot that provides a flame at your fingertips without danger, noise, or caps. Miniature batteries make it work, and an adjustable finger clip makes it more convenient for your own use. It can be reloaded in about five seconds for a repeat. This is a great way to perform small productions and to get attention at any point in your act. Many uses. Not sold to minors.

$8.50

Theater Effects, Inc.
P.O. Box 293
South Bound Brook, N.J. 08880

CANE TO FLASH WAND

You walk onstage holding your cane outright. Immediately it changes into a silk and a wand that shoots a ball of fire on your command. Spectacular! The wand has chrome tips and a chrome cap, is battery-operated, silent, and of high-quality workmanship.

This effect requires the use of the German vanishing cane, which many magicians already have. It is not sold to minors.

Wand $28.50
Cane $24.50
Set of each $49

Theater Effects, Inc.
P.O. Box 293
South Bound Brook, N.J. 08880

RAINBOW WATER ILLUSION

Now you can do something straight out of Frank Garcia's act, one of the best in the magical world today.

Imagine that you are standing in the middle of a cluster of people, and you pick up a newspaper, open it, and show both sides. Then you fold up the paper and pour a full glass of water into it. When the paper is unfolded again it is shown front, back, upside down, right side up—and the water has vanished completely.

Then the newspaper is refolded and you proceed to pour four different-colored drinks into four champagne glasses. The paper is again shown to be empty, folded, and tossed aside.

This effect is truly elegant and impressive. You get the newspaper, the secret things you'll need, and four champagne glasses.

$10

Jose's Studio
17-C Wallace St.
Belleville, N.J. 07109

FLAME-O

Suddenly a great burst of flame appears in your hand. You can blow it out and have it appear again. You reach under a silk and produce a flame, or put the flame into an egg bag and produce a dove.

This is exciting and fascinating to see, but is safe and easy to do. You must be at least eighteen years old to order it, however.

$9

Jose's Studio
17-C Wallace St.
Belleville, N.J. 07109

FORGETFUL FREDDIE

Children will get a big laugh and a lot of fun out of this one. It's an old-time favorite that adults love too. Freddie is a poor boy who cannot even remember his own head. A little model of Freddie is shown, and the head is picked up and vanished in a silk. A balloon is used to replace his head, and when the balloon bursts Freddie's head is back in place.

This Freddie is a foot high and is made of very durable plastic especially for close-up work.

$12.50

Jose's Studio
17-C Wallace St.
Belleville, N.J. 07109

THE MAGIC CARPET

Magician shows both sides of a carpet, folds it in half, and slips a dove inside. In a flash the carpet is opened flat and out flies—a silk!

This is a handy way to change small silks to large ones, to change knotted silks for unknotted ones, etc. There are many ways this can be used in your act when something needs to appear or disappear.

The carpet measures 15×26 inches and works without the necessity of hiding things in your clothes. You can even use it close to people, it is so well made.

$16

Jose's Studio
17-C Wallace St.
Belleville, N.J. 07109

FANTASIO CANE TO SILK

Fantasio appeared five times on the old *Ed Sullivan Show*, and this was always one of his most popular effects. Like all of his canes, these are made of unbreakable polyester film on the outside and will not rust, wear out, make noise, or present any other problems.

You stroll onstage, reach forward, and instantly a full-sized cane appears at your fingertips. Alternately, you have a large silk which instantly changes to a cane. Comes in a case with detailed instructions. Specify whether you want the cane in red, green, white, or basic black. The cane that appears resembles an authentic formal walking stick and comes with an interchangeable tip for use with silks or feather bouquets.

$15

International Magic
7370 N.W. 72nd Ave.
Miami, Fla. 33166

FANTASIO DANCING CANE

The solid cane in your hands begins to jump around and dance with no visible supports, then changes to any silk you provide. The cane is very lightweight. The carefully designed Mylar ring that is required is unbreakable and can be used with any cane.

$2

International Magic
7370 N.W. 72nd Ave.
Miami, Fla. 33166

FANTASIO VANISHING CANE TO SILKS

At any time in your act you twirl a cane between your fingers, tap it on the floor to prove it is solid, then hold it by both ends, and it instantly changes to two large silks (not supplied).

$9

International Magic
7370 N.W. 72nd Ave.
Miami, Fla. 33166

FANTASIO COLOR-CHANGING CANE TO SILKS

Before the vanishing effect you can change the color of the cane. Then it vanishes and changes into silks, ribbons, or whatever. State what color combination you want for the cane.

$17

International Magic
7370 N.W. 72nd Ave.
Miami, Fla. 33166

FANTASIO TRIPLE COLOR-CHANGING CANE TO SILKS

As you hold the cane in both hands and twirl it, the cane changes from black to red and then green, finally changing into two large silks (not supplied). This won four awards at two leading magic conventions in 1968.

$25

International Magic
7370 N.W. 72nd Ave.
Miami, Fla. 33166

FANTASIO VANISHING CANDLE TO SILK

You display a 15-inch candle and light it. Then you touch the flame and it disappears instantly, changing into a silk. Available in red or white, as you request.

$9

International Magic
7370 N.W. 72nd Ave.
Miami, Fla. 33166

FANTASIO VANISHING LIT CANDLE

A 15-inch candle is seen in its holder. You cover it with a silk, light the candle, and they see it burning a hole in the silk. You remove the candle and silk together from the holder—and the candle vanishes. Specify red or white.

$16

International Magic
7370 N.W. 72nd Ave.
Miami, Fla. 33166

FANTASIO COLOR-CHANGING VANISHING CANDLE

You display a 15-inch red candle and light it. When you touch the flame with your fingertips, it changes to white and is still lit. As a climax, it vanishes or changes into a silk. This set includes two candles and an adapter ring. Any holder or silk will do.

$15

International Magic
7370 N.W. 72nd Ave.
Miami, Fla. 33166

FANTASIO CANDLE TO BOUQUET

A 15-inch candle and holder is displayed. The candle is lit and changes to an 18-inch bouquet of large feather flowers with five red blooms. This comes with the candle and a deluxe chromed metal holder, plus a vase for the bouquet and everything else that is necessary. Specify red or white candle.

$40

International Magic
7370 N.W. 72nd Ave.
Miami, Fla. 33166

THE FANTASIO CANDELABRA

A candelabra is shown holding four candles. One is lighted and a 24-inch silk is produced from the flame. This candle is removed, covered by the silk, and vanishes. A second candle is lit and removed from the holder. Instantly it changes to a second silk.

The silk is displayed and the two remaining candles are covered with it. These are lit and the audience can see through the silk to know that they are burning and can see them even burning holes in the silk. The candles are removed from the holder and simultaneously both lit candles vanish.

This comes with four candles (specify red or white), a silvery candelabra, two specially prepared silks, and the entire routine as performed on the *Ed Sullivan Show*.

$50

International Magic
7370 N.W. 72nd Ave.
Miami, Fla. 33166

DAY-LITE PRODUCTION TUBES

The square circle is a well-known method of producing a quantity of items from a supposedly empty tube. In this version, both the box and the tube that fits inside are round. Anyone who thinks he is one of the "wise guys" will never figure out this one.

A beautifully decorated pair of tubes are shown. One fits inside the other, and you produce a massive amount that seems to be larger than the two tubes put together. Yards and yards of silks can be used for a beautiful effect.

This new model is self-contained and requires nothing to be hidden in your clothes, on a table, etc. The method used for this is so clever, so daring, you won't believe it even after you have seen it—especially since you seem to be able to look right through the cut-out decorations in the side of the tubes and see them empty.

$15

Aladdin Magic Shop
110 S. High St.
Columbus, Ohio 43215

RISING, FLOATING, VANISHING GLASS

A glass of liquid is covered by a fancy cloth that is 18 inches square. It clings to the fingers in defiance of gravity. It floats into space, down to the floor, and up to the fingertips again.

After it has floated around for a while you grasp the corner of the cloth and toss it high into the air. The glass, filled with liquid, has disappeared!

This is a wonderful pocket-size version of the famous Asrah levitation in which a woman, covered with a sheet, levitates and vanishes. It is visible magic, and easy to do. Nothing pleases the crowd so much as a miracle that happens in front of their very eyes, and this is a dilly.

$8

Aladdin Magic Shop
110 S. High St.
Columbus, Ohio 43215

RED, WHITE, AND BLUE

Two white blocks, two red ones, and two blue ones are shown on all sides, covered with a small cardboard tube, and they are discovered to behave in a very unusual and unlikely manner.

The magician makes two stacks of blocks, one red-white-blue and one blue-white-red. One of the cardboard tubes is unfolded and placed over one of the stacks, which is then shown to have reversed itself, so that both stacks are now in the same order.

A stack is inverted and placed in the tube, and again it shows up in reversed order. Finally, one of the stacks is tied with a ribbon, both stacks are covered with tubes, and then the tubes are removed to show the stacks in a brand-new order—one has blue-white-blue and the other red-white-red. And the ribbon that was tied is still in place! Again, the tubes can be shown to be empty.

This is a simple and straightforward-looking effect. The cardboard tubes fold flat and can be inspected. In fact, when this is done the magician never gives any cause of suspicion and will leave the spectators scratching their heads.

$40

Tom Fitzgerald
2814 Washington St.
Wilmington, Del. 19802

CONFETTI BOWLS

Two bowls with a shiny copper finish are displayed and nested on the table mouth downward. The top one is removed and shown to be empty. It is then filled with confetti. The other is inverted on top of it, and when the bowls are parted, the confetti has doubled in quantity.

Again the confetti is leveled, and an empty bowl inverted over the top. This time the bowls are parted to reveal them filled with silks, flowers, or candy (not supplied). This is an attractive version of the classic Chinese rice-bowl routine.

$7.50

Aladdin Magic Shop
110 S. High St.
Columbus, Ohio 43215

CRYSTAL CYLINDER AND CHEST

Here is a fancy-looking and surprising variation on the usual chest (or box) and cylinder productions. An attractive Chinese box is shown empty, and a clear plastic cylinder is placed in the top so that the open end sticks up above the level of the chest.

Open the door and the tube is full of silks, a live dove, whatever you want. The cylinder is shown around and the box is again shown all around.

That inventive genius U.F. Grant, who has probably devised as many new tricks and as much new apparatus as anyone living, has a routine with this that you will enjoy using. He puts the cylinder in the box and leaves the door open. The tube visibly fills with Ping-Pong balls. He closes the door, drapes a silk over the top, and removes the cylinder under this silk cover. The cabinet is shown empty. The silk is removed, and the tube is shown empty also. Then the tube is put back in the cabinet and again filled with Ping-Pong balls.

This is an attractive outfit that can be used for the above and for many other effects that you will have fun creating for your own magic show.

$24

Aladdin Magic Shop
110 S. High St.
Columbus, Ohio 43215

BRILLIANT MAGIC LAMP

This is one that will make a sensation in your living room or onstage. You call attention to a table lamp and light it up. Using the trick milk pitcher or glass described elsewhere, you pour milk into a paper bag or cone, then crush the paper to show that it has vanished. Where did it go?

Suddenly the light goes out. You remove the shade and show that it is empty, and that there is nothing wrong with the shade. But the bulb is full of milk! You unscrew the bulb, pour out the milk, and put the bulb back in the lamp, where it lights up as usual!

Water or colored liquid may be poured from the bulb instead of milk. Another possible effect is to vanish a silk and discover it inside the bulb. You can work this close-up and surrounded, and you can use your own inventive genius to come up with still other possible effects with this remarkable lamp.

$40

Aladdin Magic Shop
110 S. High St.
Columbus, Ohio 43215

THE DUTCH KIDS

Here's a nice effect for children's shows. A Dutch boy and girl are shown. She is put into a cupboard, and he is put into a box. But she has accidentally been put in upside down. Strangely, whatever happens to her also happens to him. He is standing on his head in the box.

She is turned right side up, and he appears right side up also. At last he vanishes and turns up hiding in the closet with her.

The apparatus is colorful and interesting, and the effect is really a whole routine that can be performed for small shows or large ones.

$50

Tom Fitzgerald
2814 Washington St.
Wilmington, Del. 19802

ROPE GIMMICK

If you do rope magic, these are ideal. They are screw-type devices that can be inserted inside the ends of a rope so that the joint is invisible except when seen very close-up. The brass is designed to hold the rope together securely, but also separates quickly when you desire.

The instructions include descriptions of a number of tricks with details for working them. The cut-and-restored rope and walking through a single rope are two that you may like. Some require two gimmicks.

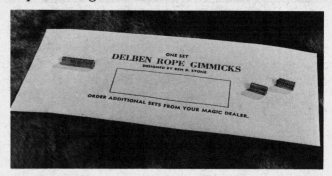

$2.50 each
$6 for three

Delben Co.
P.O. Box 3535
Springfield, Mo. 65804

I'LL BE SWITCHED

Two light bulbs and two switches are mounted on a board. The cord is plugged into a 115-volt AC outlet. You show that the switch on the right controls the light on the left, and vice versa. The reason it works that way, you explain, is that the thing was miswired. So you correct the problem by unscrewing both light bulbs and exchanging them in their sockets. Now the switch on the right controls the light on the right, etc.!

$45

Delben Co.
P.O. Box 3535
Springfield, Mo. 65804

$10

Delben Co.
P.O. Box 3535
Springfield, Mo. 65804

HYDROSTATIC MILK BOTTLE

An old-fashioned milk bottle is filled with liquid and inverted. The liquid stays suspended until you want it to gush out. These are made from bottles found by diligently searching antique stores, so the supply varies.

MAGIC SALT

Here's a little item that gets funnier the more you use it. Whenever you want to vanish something you reach in your pocket and pull out a clear plastic salt shaker and sprinkle some salt on the object. Then you make the object disappear or do whatever you were going to do with it. But the salt shaker has vanished! A little later you reach in your pocket and pull it out again and go through the whole routine a second time, and as often as you like during your performance. The salt shaker keeps vanishing and reappearing.

$3

Glenn Comar
353 E. Sixth Ave.
Roselle, N.J. 07203

AM INK

You borrow a pen from someone, give it a slight twist, and music starts playing from the pen. Or you draw a picture of a radio, pretend to turn it on, and your favorite program is actually heard. This can be performed immediately.

$20

Al's Magic Shop
1205 Pennsylvania Ave. N.W.
Washington, D.C. 20004

WATER SUSPENSION

Use a soft drink or beer bottle containing water. Turn the bottle over, and nothing comes out. You can put matches or other objects into the mouth of the bottle while it is inverted, yet still nothing comes out.

$1

Flosso Hornmann
304 W. 34th St.
New York, N.Y. 10001

THE FAMOUS EGG BAG

Tricks may come and tricks may go, but the magic of the egg bag is eternal. For such is the fate of the truly popular.

The magician shows an attractive bag, inside and out. He places an egg inside the bag, and upon pronouncing the mystic words, causes it to disappear. The bag is turned inside out, banged upon a table, and, in short, everything done to prove the actual disappearance of the egg. Yet when the magician places his hand in the bag, he produces the vanished egg.

As a special favor to the audience, the magician fully and carefully explains (?) how the trick is done. Then, following his every move, convinced that they are "in the know," the audience soon discovers the magician has completely fooled them and left them more mystified than before. The bag is again shown empty, and even felt by the spectators, two of whom are then requested to hold the performer's wrists. Whereupon he reaches into the bag and produces the missing egg, which may again be vanished and changed into a baby chick or any other object.

Of high-quality manufacture and materials, the egg bag comes to you complete with an easy-to-do routine that's full of comedy situations. Special egg supplied.

$3

Warner's Magic Factory
Box 455
Hinsdale, III. 60521

COLOR SYMPHONY

This is without a doubt one of the most beautiful effects in magic.

A stand with four 45-rpm phonograph records is on a table. You show a record jacket to be absolutely empty, pick up one of the records, show it on both sides, and insert it into the jacket. You next pick up a red silk hanky and thread it through the spindle hole in the center of the record. When you remove the record from the jacket, it has changed to the color of the silk, red. The record is shown to be red on both sides and then returned to the record stand. The jacket is shown to be absolutely empty.

The same thing is repeated with the second and third records, changing them to yellow and blue respectively. The three colored silk hankies are threaded together through the last record and it changes into a tri-color record.

But that's not all. For a finale, the four colored records are picked up and held in the hand. They are covered with a black silk and then removed, one by one, in their original black color.

Records are shown on both sides before and after each color change, and record jacket is shown empty at the start, in between every color change, and at the end. It may even be torn into pieces at the end. The silks are absolutely un-gimmicked and may be used for other effects either before or after this effect. Real records are used.

Complete with records, silks, jackets, stand, etc. A full routine is provided.

$24.50

James Rainho Products
14 Windsor Rd.
Medford, Mass. 02155

TUMBLE DOWN

A tube is shown to be absolutely empty and a glass (plastic tumbler) is run through it. The tube is placed on the table and covered with a book, sheet of glass or plastic, etc. A silk hanky is draped over the book, and the glass on a coaster is placed on top of the hanky. Another hanky is draped over the glass, and the magician begins to press down on the covered glass. The glass form is seen to slowly sink downward, going right through the book. The top hanky is whisked away to reveal only the coaster on top of the bottom hanky. The glass is found inside the tube on the table.

$10

James Rainho Products
14 Windsor Rd.
Medford, Mass. 02155

DEHYDRATED MILK PITCHER

The pitcher is made of crystal-clear plastic. It is shown to be full of milk. The performer explains that most milk contains over 90 percent water and only 10 percent *real* milk. To prove this, he takes an ordinary shot glass, then proceeds to pour the *entire contents* of the pitcher into the glass! Thus the liquid has *visibly* shrunk! Contents of the shot glass are then poured back into the pitcher to show exactly *how much* milk was lost in the dehydrating process. Can be used for many other effects—vanishing milk into a folded piece of newspaper, for example, or pouring it into a boy's ear.

$2.50

Magic and Fun
P.O. Box 1936
Grand Central Station
New York, N.Y. 10017

SUPER NEEDLE BALLOON

The performer displays a large clear balloon, which can be blown up by the spectator. A very long needle with a ribbon threaded through the eyelet is offered for careful examination. Without hesitation, the performer shoves the needle through the balloon and draws the ribbon through the holes made by the needle! The balloon does not break! After withdrawing the ribbon, the balloon is then burst to show that it actually can be broken.

This effect is downright fun to do! The needle can even be left in the balloon with both ends of the needle sticking out and the spectators can be invited for a really close look. Pushing the needle into the balloon has to be one of the most unusual experiences you will encounter. It doesn't break!

No tape or prior preparation to the balloon is required—the method used in the super needle balloon is entirely new.

The needle is extremely sharp and dangerous. Definitely not for kids!

$6.50

Accent Products
1550 West Dr.
Walled Lake, Mich. 48088

NO TICKEE, NO SHIRTEE

The performer exhibits a long strip of paper bearing Chinese characters. The ticket is shown on *both* sides. The hands are empty. The magician relates a story of going to his Chinese laundry for his shirt and the Chinaman tells him the shirt is not ready. Well, this gets the magician angry, so he tears the ticket into smithereens. Whereupon the laundryman says, "I play trick on you, I fool you—shirtee ready but you can't get it. No tickee, no shirtee." The magician says, "So you fool me? Now I fool you—I've got my shirtee." The magician has opened the supposedly torn pieces of ticket and exhibits a shirt. Simple, self-contained.

Twelve tickets $2

Magic and Fun
P.O. Box 1936
Grand Central Station
New York, N.Y. 10017

AIRBORNE GLASS

Great visual magic! Performer displays a glass and a bottle of soda pop. He begins to pour the liquid into the glass. Very casually he lets go of the glass and continues to pour into the glass. The glass, filling with liquid, remains suspended in midair.

Hard to believe—but true. Use any bottle of pop, any liquid, no attachments to the performer's body. You'll love this one and surely make it a regular feature of your act.

$3

Warner's Magic Factory
Box 455
Hinsdale, Ill. 60521

MULTI-COLOR PAPER PRODUCTION—MAXIMILIANO LONDONO

The effect with which Londono startled the magic world—a "do-as-I-do" routine in which the magician and spectator both tear up a white strip of tissue paper and begin to stuff it in mouth. The magician then pulls from his mouth yards of multi-colored paper. A riot of laughs follows as the spectator removes only the few pieces of white tissue paper. A spectacular magic effect. Supplied with package of twelve garlands and complete instructions.

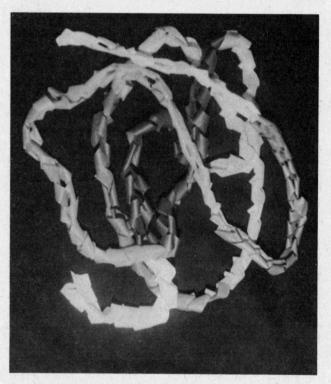

$4

Guaranteed Magic
27 Bright Rd.
Hatboro, Pa. 19040

ANIMAL ANTICS

The most famous small stage illusion is the appearance of a rabbit from a borrowed hat that has previously been shown to be empty. Interestingly enough, the connection between magicians and rabbits goes back at least as far as the mid-1700s, when a woman named Mary Toft pretended to have given birth to a number of rabbits.

She was the wife of a journeyman clothworker named Joshua Tofts, and lived in the English country of Surrey at the time. A contemporary description says she was of "a healthy strong constitution, small size, fair complexion, very stupid and sullen temper and unable to read or write." Nonetheless, she managed to convince a local surgeon, John Howard, of her unlikely story, and also the king's medical adviser and a number of other doctors. It is not clear what proofs she came up with that were so convincing, but she did get a lot of testimony on her behalf.

Finally a German court physician to George III traipsed out into the country to discover the truth, since he was suspicious and doubtful of the stories he had heard. Not surprisingly, he came back to tell his majesty that it was a hoax after all. Some people were not a bit surprised, and the woman later even confessed. Meanwhile, a London magician had become inspired and had new posters distributed all over the city

to announce his latest illusion, "The Birth of a Rabbit."

In performance, he talked about Mrs. Toft's improbable offspring and borrowed a top hat from someone in the audience. He placed it crown down on a table top, made a few magical passes over it, and pulled out a gorgeous white rabbit, alive and kicking. The crowd loved it.

The hat trick was brought to its greatest perfection by Joseph Michael Harts in the middle of the last century. Using a small, unadorned table, he was able to take a borrowed hat and draw forth large bandannas, ten pint goblets, fifty cigars, champagne bottles, fifteen packs of cards, a life-sized Japanese baby doll, a crinoline petticoat, a silver cage with a live canary inside, a hundred yards of ribbon, a papier-mâché skull, and seven lighted lanterns. The act went on for twenty-two minutes and the performer never left the stage during that time.

Later Howard Thurston added the idea of producing inflated balloons, and Harry Stork produced sizzling fried oysters, but neither such oddities nor Harts' voluminous production ever matched the appeal of the single white rabbit.

Interestingly, rabbits are not the most popular livestock to be produced by magicians. The honor goes to doves. The best-known effects involving birds are the dove pan, in which a shallow pan with a lid is shown and filled with flames before the birds are released; and the vanishing birdcage, in which the birds disappear, cage and all, in front of the audience. The cage was invented by the great French artist Bautier de Kolta in the second half of the last century. De Kolta also invented spring-loaded flowers and the vanishing-lady illusion.

There is no doubt that the appearance of a live animal is always impressive—and so is vanishing it into thin air. But if you are going to include livestock in your act you must take proper care of the animals. The cruelty to animals attributed to some magicians would not be tolerated by today's audiences.

If you choose to work with animals, the effects can be stunning. Doug Henning created news by transforming a woman into a caged tiger. Blackstone vanished a horse, and the great Houdini's feat was to vanish an elephant. But the size of the effect is not as important as the presentation.

W. J. Nixon is the inventor of a wonderful little effect that he calls "Where do the ducks go?" The performer takes three ducks out of a wicker cage, puts them in a box, and closes the lid. The ducks vanish and the box is promptly taken apart, but the audience is led to suspect the table on which the box rested. In fact, the cloth covering is removed and some feathers are seen sticking out below. These turn out to be part of a fan.

If keeping animals is not possible for you, then you could work with fake animals that look real from a distance. Or you could substitute stuffed animals and play for a comic effect.

Many magicians have become very attached to their animals, however. A particularly devoted animal owner was Siegmund Neuberger, who performed under the name Lafayette. Given a mongrel dog called Beauty by Harry Houdini, Lafayette used the dog's picture on his checks and in all of his advertising. A large metal plaque in front of his house bore the animal's likeness and the inscription, "The more I see of men, the more I love my dog."

Beauty was pampered with a full *table d'hote* dinner each evening, complete from soup to dessert, and a butler even tucked a napkin into the dog's diamond-studded collar. Lafayette was the soul of hospitality to people as well, but in his dining room hung the motto, "You may drink my wine, eat my food, command my servants—but you must respect my dog." He was so devoted to the animal that once, in Louisville, Ky., he refused to go onstage to a full house when his dog was missing.

"Don't ring up the curtain," he said. "I must find my Beauty." The manager protested: "Would you ruin me?" The magician snapped back, "Yes! If that's the price of recovering my dog." He ordered his treasurer to pay the manager the amount of money necessary to refund every admission that had been sold that night.

In May 1911, the dog died of apoplexy in Edinburgh, and its remains were embalmed. Barely a week later, Lafayette himself perished in a theater fire. The most elaborate of all the floral tributes that came was from Houdini, who had florists working day and night to complete a model of Beauty lying upon a cushion of flowers. His accompanying card said simply, "To the memory of my friend from the friend who gave him his best friend, Beauty."

CHERRY

For those who want to perform an act with animals but are unable to undertake the care and feeding of any little creatures, this is an unbelievably real-looking rabbit. Quality workmanship and design make it seem to be alive, even from a short distance.

$30

Tom Fitzgerald
2814 Washington St.
Wilmington, Del. 19802

TWIN DOVES IN BALLOON

A pagoda is displayed as being empty. A balloon is inflated into the opening, the pagoda is shown on both sides, and one-two-three, the balloon bursts and two doves make their appearance. This may be done surrounded by the audience! Complete instructions, pagoda, and a supply of balloons are included; you supply the doves.

$35

Deratzian Magical Enterprises
922 Spring Ave.
Troy, N. Y. 12180

$37.50

Jose's Studio
17-C Wallace St.
Belleville, N.J. 07109

IMPROVED BUNNY BOX

Here is a novel way of making a rabbit or anything else come to life. It can be worked so close the spectator can actually be holding the box when it occurs. Yet is easy to do surrounded.

You take a slate and draw a rabbit, dove, flower, or some silks on it. You place the slide in the back of the box. The two front doors of the box are then opened and the slate is shown. The box is otherwise perfectly empty. The doors are closed, a "magic" word is uttered. The top and front doors are opened. The drawing has come to life!

The box is made of durable Masonite with a glossy finish. The dimensions are 8×10×12 inches.

INDIAN DOVE CHEST

Decorated with dancing American Indians in feathered headdress, this 12-inch-square chest sits on a table base and holds as many as five doves. When the top is removed and the four sides are dropped, the doves have vanished completely. In their place, there is a cat or rabbit or inflated balloons, or anything else you want.

It can be worked close-up and surrounded.

$75

Aladdin Magic Shop
110 S. High St.
Columbus, Ohio 43215

Before

After

VANISHING AQUARIUM

The magician displays a beautiful chrome-trimmed aquarium in which live fish are swimming playfully. He removes a couple of fish with a little net and gives them away to a spectator. He now takes the aquarium in his hands, tosses it in the air, and it visibly vanishes. This is a real stunner done without any covering!

$44

Danny Korem
417 Tiffany Trail
Richardson, Tex. 75080

DOVE CLASSIC

You show your hands are empty—before removing a handkerchief from your breast pocket and spreading it over one hand. The hanky is whipped away, and in your hand is a beautiful live white dove. This is modern magic at its best. At the end of the act you may repeat the effect and produce a second dove. Complete instructions and equipment are included—but no dove.

NITE-CLUB DOVE VANISH

A dove is placed in a fancy chest, which is then taken apart piece by piece. Both sides of each piece are shown. The dove has vanished! There are no threads, no doves dangling precariously from underneath. This can be done close-up, surrounded, and without a table which makes it ideal for a night-club act.

$25

Aladdin Magic Shop
110 S. High St.
Columbus, Ohio 43215

$4

Flosso Hornmann
304 W. 34th St.
New York, N.Y. 10001

DAGGER LIVESTOCK VANISH

A very attractive chest is open at the front and top. It is freely shown and may be handled by anyone. A member of the audience can even step up and place a pair of doves or a rabbit in the chest.

The front panel is put into place to hide the livestock, and you push a large wooden dagger right through the center of the chest. The front panel is removed and shown on all sides. The chest is empty! You can now pick it up, using the dagger as a handle, and show it all around.

The chest is 10×8×6 inches and is solidly built. The audience can watch from any angle and still the vanish occurs. No assistants needed, and it's foolproof.

$25

Aladdin Magic Shop
110 S. High St.
Columbus, Ohio 43215

FLIP-OVER BOX

This is the perfect box for the perfect livestock disappearance! It is probably the best method invented to vanish small birds and animals.

What you get is a new and handsomely decorated box measuring 8¼×6×4 inches. It is beautiful and durable with large, solid hinges on all doors for long life.

What happens? You simply put the animals inside a box shaped like a cigar box. The top and bottom lids fall open when you spin the box in your fingers, so people can look through and see an empty inside. The livestock has promptly vanished into thin air! Instructions are included.

$39.50

Lou Tannen
1540 Broadway
New York, N.Y. 10036

DOVE PRODUCTION ROYALE

This is one of the cleanest and most convincing ways to magically produce doves. A single silk is shown. It is twisted, twirled, shown freely on both sides. Then it is bunched up, and from it flutters a real live dove.

This method has a number of advantages, and does not require a lot of the usual hocus pocus. Because of the large number of possible ways to use this, the instructions that are included offer a large number of suggestions.

The beautiful foulard is like an ordinary silk, except in a heavier weight to last longer. You can also use ordinary silks if you desire. You can produce flowers, silks, or streamers with this prop.

$7.50

Lou Tannen
1540 Broadway
New York, N.Y. 10036

DOVE PLATES

This is completely different from the famous dove pan illusion and in many ways more impressive.

You take two ordinary plates without any preparation. They can be examined. One plate is filled with confetti, and to show that even the confetti is unprepared it is showered down from one plate into the other. Put the second plate upside down on the first filled with confetti. When the top plate is removed the confetti has vanished. Sitting on the plate are two live doves.

The audience can see the plates at all times. This is a completely open and amazing dove production that can be done in the middle of a crowd.

$15

Tom Fitzgerald
2814 Washington St.
Wilmington, Del. 19802

MANDARIN CABINET

This attractive cabinet, highly decorated in five colors, is used to produce any kind of small livestock. You can open two side doors so that the audience can look through and see the cabinet empty. The top is also held open for inspection. The box is put on the stand. The doors are closed. The magician reaches in through the top and begins producing doves or a rabbit or any other small animal.

$48

Healey's Magic Co.
1612 Dickson Ave.
Scranton, Pa. 18509

SLINKY SNAKE

A card is chosen, then placed back in the deck. The deck is thrown on the floor and the snake picks out the correct card. This is just one of many tricks the snake does. Over 4 feet long, Slinky is made of two-color sponge-ball material. It has lovely fangs, glowing eyes, leash and collar. Pet rocks just sit, but pet snake slithers anywhere you wish, provides real action. Routine and funny patter included.

$5

Stanley Blumenthal
14608 Greenleaf St.
Sherman Oaks, Cal. 91403

DOVE PAN

This prop has 1001 uses and is limited only by your imagination. It is a beautiful piece of quality equipment and superb craftsmanship that you will be proud to own. This is the standard means of producing doves.

One of the many effects possible is this one: You show the pan empty, break an egg into it, and add salt, pepper, and some lighter fluid. In goes a lit match and up go the flames. The cover is dropped into position to put out the flames, and then immediately removed. The pan is then seen to contain two doves or a small rabbit. Or candy or cake can fill the pan.

Though this attractive pan looks small it will hold a large amount. It is made of high-quality aluminum and is light in weight and sturdy, with a quick release to allow the hidden objects or livestock to appear instantly. It is 8 inches in diameter and 5 inches high. The dove pan rests on three ball-like supports and is buffed, polished, and lacquered.

This is a piece of professional magic apparatus designed for the working magician who will give it years of wear and who will feature it prominently in his act. A quality product.

$18

Lou Tannen
1540 Broadway
New York, N.Y. 10036

DOUBLE-LOAD DOVE PAN

Same as the regular dove pan, only after the first production occurs you put the lid on the table and you are ready to make a second surprise production as large as the first one.

$22.50

Lou Tannen
1540 Broadway
New York, N.Y. 10036

RABBIT LOADER

The production of a live rabbit, guinea pig, pair of doves, etc., from a handful of silks is a great

It begins with a nicely made and decorated cage about 15×10×10 inches. Two doves are placed inside and visibly change to two white silks, silently fluttering from feathery reality to silken surprise.

The apparatus is safe for the birds and works automatically. It can also be used for other effects. Doves not included.

$42.50

Lou Tannen
1540 Broadway
New York, N.Y. 10036

DOVE OF PEACE

Two tall cylinders are shown empty before being nested. A large supply of silks are produced from nested cylinders. Colors that match national flags are used. These silks are placed in a clear plastic cylinder, which is pushed up through the nested cylinders to emerge with a live dove in place of the silks. This is a very attractive and unexpected effect.

$15

Aladdin Magic Shop
110 S. High St.
Columbus, Ohio 43215

effect that has been performed by many of the greatest names in magic.

The usual effect is that a great number of silks, streamers, and so on are produced magically from a box or tube by any means the magician wishes. As the silks are produced, they are draped over a chair. The magician picks them up and walks forward with them, holds the silks over a table or tray for a moment, and then makes the livestock appear.

The method presented here is one that can be used like the above, or with an assistant away from all objects on the stage. It can be used to make the livestock appear from a newspaper, a hat, and so on. Included in the necessary secret equipment used to load up the hat or silks is something that not only holds the animals safely until wanted, but which frees them instantly. Detailed instructions are included.

$12.50

Lou Tannen
1540 Broadway
New York, N.Y. 10036

DOVE-TO-SILK CAGE

Any time the word "dove" appears in the name of an effect used by magicians, other kinds of birds or small animals can probably be used. In this case, however, doves do work especially well.

THE BENGAL NET

The Bengal net consists of a rod with a hanging banner. Hanging in front of the banner is a net, which is folded in half and hooked into position to form a hammock of sorts.

A pair of doves, a large rabbit, or anything it will hold is placed in the net. At your command the net falls open and the items therein visibly vanish. The banner is moved out of the way to allow the audience to see through the net. There is no question that the pair of doves or rabbit has vanished.

This new design allows the vanish to take place with only one hand being used. Can be worked as part of a close-up act if you wish, since it does not matter if you are surrounded.

Large deluxe size $40

Aladdin Magic Shop
110 S. High St.
Columbus, Ohio 43215

INSTANT DOVE

Picture this! A beautiful 24-inch silk foulard is produced or merely picked up by performer and held by its corner; it is shown unmistakably empty from all sides. The magician then grasps the opposite corner in his other hand and holds the silk outstretched and again shows both sides of the cloth. At no time do the performer's hands approach his body. At the performer's command a live dove flutters and appears perched on the center of the top edge of the silk. The magician's hands are approximately 10 inches from the dove on each side when it is produced. Comes complete.

$20

Healey's Magic Co.
1612 Dickson Ave.
Scranton, Pa. 18509

FINAL RABBIT VANISH

You open the lid of a box and put in a rabbit. Immediately the top is removed and shown on both sides. Then each side is removed, shown, and put aside. On top of the bottom of the box is a "lump" under a cloth. You look embarrassed because the rabbit has not yet vanished. But when the cloth is removed, there sits a gorgeous bouquet of flowers in a small pot. This is picked up and placed aside. Then the base of the box is shown. The rabbit is gone!

You do not have to sneak away the rabbit when no one is looking, and there are no wires, no switching one box for another. You don't hide things in your clothes. This outfit is completely self-contained, and comes complete with a gorgeous take-apart box, the cloth, pot, and fifty of the biggest and most beautiful pop-up flowers you have ever seen.

$70

Healey's Magic Co.
1612 Dickson Ave.
Scranton, Pa. 18509

DOUBLE-DOVE PENETRATION

A colorfully decorated plastic tube is shown to be completely empty. Then two doves are placed inside, and they really fill the tube so that there is not an inch of space to spare. Caps are placed over the ends of the tube and sixteen assorted knives and spikes are pushed through the tube. They go in at various angles. There is no way that the doves can escape being skewered unless they have vanished.

The knives and spikes are removed, the caps are removed, and the tube is uncovered so the doves can be removed. They emerge unhurt from the container. Even when you know the secret, you'll swear it can't be done. The tube, caps, knives, spikes, and instructions are provided—everything but the livestock.

$69.50

Lou Tannen
1540 Broadway
New York, N.Y. 10036

FLAGS

A small, multi-colored strip of paper is passed from hand to hand in the audience. It is torn in half and then in half again. Everyone thinks they are going to see a torn-and-restored paper trick, but not quite! The paper pieces are crumpled into a ball, which immediately becomes a string of beautiful large silk flags from various countries. The magician holds the string of flags across his body with both arms outstretched.

But that's just the beginning. Doves, silks, or what-have-you can then be produced from the flags. This makes an interesting and unexpected opening effect.

$5

Guaranteed Magic
27 Bright Rd.
Hatboro, Pa. 19040

DOUBLE-PARAKEET BAG

A cloth bag is shown to be empty beyond doubt. The magician sticks his hand into the bag and out come two parakeets resting on his palm.

$10.90

Elmo Magic Supreme
1753 E. 16th St.
Brooklyn, N.Y. 11229

DOVE FROM POSTER

Here's a great way to open your act! You, or your assistant, display a full-sized 20×30-inch poster, all in color, depicting "Dove Deceptions."

The poster is folded and immediately a live fluttering dove is produced. Nothing is hidden in your clothes.

$3

Glenn Comar
353 E. Sixth Ave.
Roselle, N.J. 07203

RABBIT IN THE HAT

This cute little bunny lives in its own magic top hat. It's a lively, happy, friendly companion, great at a children's party. And, there are a number of magic tricks which the bunny can do by itself. (Well, almost!) It is an act by itself.

Everything is included—rabbit, hat, manuscript of tips and ideas, even some tricks and props for the rabbit to use.

$30

Warner's Magic Factory
Box 455
Hinsdale, Ill. 60521

TOP HAT "SURPRISE"

Now at last a paper tear that will win you much applause from both adults and children.

You show two pieces of tissue, one black and one white. These are torn to make four. Now the four are torn to make eight; the eight pieces are rolled into a ball in the hands. When you open the wad of paper it is seen that the white tissue has vanished and the ball is all black. When you open the ball of tissue, the black has joined together to form a magician's black top hat. This is really a magical top hat, and upon reaching into it, you produce yards of black and white tissue in the form of a chain.

Finally the chain ends and you state if this is truly a magician's top hat you may be able to produce a rabbit. When you give another tug on the chain a cute white rabbit appears in the hat. The whole thing can be given to a spectator as a gift or for helping you do the trick. No sleights—this is a great self-contained paper tear.

$7

Jack Miller Enterprises
119 Weymouth Rd.
Syracuse, N.Y. 13205

BREAK-APART VANISH

Another amazing vanishing trick. Place your doves in this break-apart and say the magic word. Then pull apart the pieces, showing that the doves have vanished—right before your very eyes.

The break-apart is easy to assemble and built to last. It measures 12×12×6 inches.

$17.50

Zanadu
165 Hancock Ave.
Jersey City, N.J. 07307

NEWSPAPER TAKE-APART VANISH

A dove is placed inside a chest in which the sides, top, and bottom frames are covered with sheets of newspaper. All at once, each side is removed and impaled on an assistant's arm, proving the panels are free of trickery. The front panel is left until last, so naturally the audience thinks the dove is hidden there. But the newspaper is broken in this panel also, proving that the dove has truly vanished.

ATOMIC DOVE VANISH PLANS

A large box consisting of top and four thin, separate side sections is first built up on a thin-topped undraped table. Four or five doves are then placed into the box through a hinged lid in the top. Immediately the box is taken apart rapidly, and as each flat section is removed it is shown on both sides and then stacked flat. The table top, which has served as the bottom of the box, is then removed.

Workshop plans to build this amazing effect are offered.

$27.50

Flosso Hornmann
304 W. 34th St.
New York, N.Y. 10001

$1

Flosso Hornmann
304 W. 34th St.
New York, N.Y. 10001

 # SILKEN SORCERY

Nothing in magic is as colorful as conjuring with silk. There is something gossamer and ethereal about the shimmering colors and brilliant dyes of a magician's silks as they are mysteriously tied and untied, as they appear or vanish, as the colors change or objects become scarves and scarves become objects.

Perhaps the captivating quality of the silks is the material itself, different from silks not bought from magical suppliers. There is magic in the very way they look. Magicians use pure silk without the glaze normally found on commercial silks. This accounts for their extraordinary compressibility. A seemingly endless supply can be compacted into a very small area, hidden inside a tube, box, or other device, so that when you begin to produce the silks, you seem to go on forever, taking out far more from a small object than it could possibly hold.

Many silk effects require no special props at all, and can be found in most books on magic. Twentieth-century silks is one such effect. Three different-colored silks are knotted together at the corners and change position, or two silks are knotted together and a third one vanishes and appears tied in between the other two. Other effects, such as a silk that changes color

as you pass your hand over it, are produced by having special preparation in advance.

There are silks that are solid colors, silks that are multi-colored, and some that are printed with elaborate designs such as Chinese dragons, or comic illustrations for comedy effects. One popular effect that takes advantage of both solid-color silks and spectacular multi-colored ones is blendo, where three silks are "blended" together into one large one.

Silks can be vanished in a variety of ways, and there are many exciting methods of making them appear. One effect is to have the silk appear in an inflated balloon. Another is to have it appear inside a capped Coke bottle.

In addition to the beauty and excitement created by any use of silks and by the many spectacular and beautiful effects produced with silks, they can be an integral part of almost any other kind of feat you might wish to perform. Anytime something needs to be covered, a silk can be used—and the silk does not have to be just picked up off a stand, it can appear from midair, from an assistant's ear, from a cane that seemed to start out solid, until it collapsed visibly into silk. Everything looks far more magical when a brilliant silk is used.

4TH DIMENSION BOX KIT

This adds another dimension to your show. You open both doors to show the box is empty, then you close the doors and reach into the box from the top to produce an almost endless stream of silks. After the production, you may even hand out the box to be examined. Self-working and easy to assemble. Box measures 10×10×3 inches.

$13.50

Zanadu
165 Hancock Ave.
Jersey City, N.J. 07307

SYMPATHETIC SILKS

The performer displays six beautiful solid-color silks, which are shown to be unprepared. They are counted one at a time from one hand to the other. Three silks are tied together at the corners to make a chain. Genuine knots are used. The three knotted silks are handed to a spectator to hold.

Upon the magician's command, and without his touching any of the silks, the three knots

leave one set and pass to the other group of three. Upon examination by spectators, that is exactly what has happened! No wonder amateurs and professionals alike love this trick. Complete instructions for routines included.

Six 18-inch silks $32.50
Six 24-inch silks $57.50
Six 36-inch silks $67.50

Lou Tannen
1540 Broadway
New York, N.Y. 10036

ACROBATIC SILK

A white wand is shown to have three holes. In the left and middle holes, red handkerchiefs are passed, and in the right, a yellow one. To convince the audience that nothing is fake, one handkerchief is removed from the hole. The magician then says, "Let's exchange the handkerchief from left to right!" The performer passes the wand from the left hand to the right behind his back and shows it to the audience. It looks like the handkerchiefs have exchanged. However, if the performance is repeated several times, the audience will find out that the trick is just done by turning the wand. So, the audience thinks they know the trick. The magician does it once more, this time finding the red handkerchief in the middle exchanged with the yellow one. An amazing effect to please an audience.

$11

Magic and Fun
P.O. Box 1936
Grand Central Station
New York, N.Y. 10017

No. 412 Walsh's cane to silk $34.50
No. 413 Walsh's silk to cane $34.50

Rice's Silk King Studio
640 Evening Star Ln.
Cincinnati, Ohio 45220

EMBARRASSING SILKS

Showing two red silks, the magician states that he bought two white silks for his wife, but when he got home, he discovered the clerk at the store had given him red silks in error. He now places the red silks into an empty box, and says the magic words. When the silks are removed from box, they are white. Audience thinks red silks are in the box, so box is opened, inside out, and it's really empty! Comes complete with four silks and box.

$5

Magic and Fun
P.O. Box 1936
Grand Central Station
New York, N.Y. 10017

SIMPLY 20TH-CENTURY SILKS

Two silk hankies of similar color are pinned together with a safety pin and are placed in a tall glass or goblet. A silk hanky of a different contrasting color is then poked into the first and it changes into a golf ball, which is also placed into the glass. The silk hankies in the glass are immediately pulled out and the odd-colored silk that was changed into the golf ball is now pinned between the first two silks. There is no sign of the golf ball. No sleight-of-hand involved; it is absolutely self-contained.

The pinned hankies can be freely handled, one dangling from the other, which makes this version superior to others on the market. Comes complete with all silks and golf ball.

$11

James Rainho Products
14 Windsor Rd.
Medford, Mass. 02155

WALSH'S CANE TO SILK/SILK TO CANE

This is an excellent opening effect that can be done anywhere, anytime! A cane is proved solid, then a few flourishes are presented. Suddenly the cane vanishes, leaving a silk.

Now perform the cane trick in reverse! A white-tipped black silk vanishes and a fully extended cane appears in its place!

SILK AND MILK FANTASY

A tube is shown empty and a silk hanky is inserted into it. The corners remain on the outside and are visible to the audience. The magician blows on the tube, and the silk vanishes instantly. The tube is shown empty from both ends. The magician picks up a glass of milk and covers it momentarily with the tube. When the tube is lifted off, the milk has vanished from the glass and in its place is the silk that previously vanished. The silk is then made to change back into milk, which is poured out. The silk then appears back in the empty glass.

$8

James Rainho Products
14 Windsor Rd.
Medford, Mass. 02155

CUT AND RESTORED SILK

After showing a stiff piece of paper on both sides, the performer forms it into the shape of a tube. A silk is then pushed into the tube, until its ends protrude on both sides. The performer now uses a pair of scissors to cut the tube in half. He separates the two halves, each part of the tube still having a silk at each end. Finally, when the two halves are placed together and the silk is removed, it is seen to be fully restored. Everything is furnished, including silk, tube, etc.

$2.50

Magic and Fun
P.O. Box 1936
Grand Central Station
New York, N.Y. 10017

SILK TO FLAG

The performer shows a 12-inch red silk, then pokes it into his left fist. As quick as a flash, both hands are opened and the red silk has changed into a silk flag. The flag may be examined, as there are no pockets, etc. Requiring no skill, this pretty effect can be performed almost as soon as you receive the silk flag, red silk, and "magic vanisher."

$2

Magic and Fun
P.O. Box 1936
Grand Central Station
New York, N.Y. 10027

THE UNKNOTTING SILK

This is beyond doubt one of the spookiest effects in silk magic. A knot is tied in the center of an 18-inch silk, in view of the audience. As the silk is held at arm's length, the spectators see it untie itself right in front of their eyes!

This uncanny, "creepy" effect is really easy to do when you know the secret. Furnished with illustrated routine and an 18-inch silk.

$2.50

Magic and Fun
P.O. Box 1936
Grand Central Station
New York, N.Y. 10017

ALL BALLED UP

A long tube is shown and a red ball dropped into it. The ball rolls out of the bottom. The red ball is again dropped into the tube, but this time a red silk hanky is pulled out of the bottom.

The same thing is repeated with yellow and blue balls, changing them into yellow and blue silks. The audience suspects that the balls may still be inside the tube.

The magician is aware of this, so he eyes the audience coyly and removes another silk from the tube—this silk has the three colored balls *imprinted* on it. The tube is shown to be absolutely empty.

All silks used are ordinary and do not conceal anything. Absolutely self-contained and very easy to do. Comes complete with tube, balls, silks, and a ball stand.

$15

James Rainho Products
14 Windsor Rd.
Medford, Mass. 02155

WALTZING MATILDA

This is not just another version of the dancing hankie. This is a silk which will dance, prance, and be merry. It will glide with grace and elegance or float in an eerie and mysterious man-

ner. It can be cute or comical. It will enchant a theater audience or the guests in your living room. Every act has a spot for it, whether as a feature, fill-in, or throw-away.

There are no threads. Waltzing Matilda is strictly self-contained, a one-man effect. Pick the silk up from your table or take it out of your pocket. It starts to waltz all around. Grab the bottom and the upper part does a hula. Comes complete with silk.

$4

Guaranteed Magic
27 Bright Rd.
Hatboro, Pa. 19040

SILK IN BALLOON

This is a magical classic—the visual appearance of a vanished silk inside a large inflated transparent balloon! It looks like real magic!

The balloon is on display in a neat holder, and is removed and freely shown. Suddenly, without cover of any kind, the previously vanished silk appears in the balloon. There's no illusion about it—the silk is definitely inside the balloon!

The balloon is burst with a long steel pin and the magician immediately catches and displays the silk.

$8.50

Jack Miller Enterprises
119 Weymouth Rd.
Syracuse, N.Y. 13205

GLORPY

Here is one of the most unusual effects, and one of the easiest to perform, you'll ever see. The magician pulls a brightly colored scarf from his pocket, shows it to be empty on both sides, and folds it on the table in front of him. Then, slowly and mysteriously, a small shape rises up in the center of the cloth. It moves and bobs up and down and finally rises to a height of almost 5 inches. Then, when your audience is dying to know what is inside, you grab a corner of the handkerchief and shake it in the air—empty! Glorpy is a real mind-blower that your audience will long remember. The instructions are very easy and come with many different "patter" ideas and routines. This is fun magic to perform that people will ask you to repeat time and again.

$3.50

The Wizard
1136 Pearl St.
Boulder, Colo. 80302

RICE'S CARD SILKS

Devise your own effects for these beautiful silks. You are offered a choice of the king of spades, the jack of diamonds, or the queen of hearts, each printed on an 18-inch silk in beautiful colors, and accompanied by a matching blank silk.

The blank silk can be used to change into the chosen card in combination with revealing the card chosen by a spectator. Just make sure the spectator "freely" picks the card that matches the silk, then use a dye tube or any other means of changing the blank silk into the printed one.

$15

Rice's Silk King Studios
640 Evening Star Ln.
Cincinnati, Ohio 45220

SNIP-SNAP SILK

An unprepared silk is shown and a piece of construction paper is folded into three parts to make a sleeve. The silk is run into the sleeve until it is clearly seen sticking out each end. If you pull one end long, the other end gets short, so the audience knows the scarf is really in there.

Then you cut the sleeve in half. There is no folding, no suspicious moves, just a quick cut—snip!—and a half is held in each hand. You bring the halves together, take hold of one end of the silk, and—snap!—the silk is completely restored as the halves of the paper sleeve flutter to the floor.

This is clean-looking and effective. It's what is known in the trade as—magic!

$4.50

Lou Tannen
1540 Broadway
New York, N.Y. 10036

CANDLE TO FLOWERS

A large burning candle in an attractive 12-inch metal candlestick is extinguished and covered with a silk. As the silken cover is removed, the audience is amazed to see a large beautiful bou-

quet of flowers that is twice as high as the candle it magically replaced. A real stunner.

$175

H. Marshall & Co.
294 W. South St.
Akron, Ohio 44311

BANDS OF AFGHAN

The performer exhibits a band of muslin cloth, about 24 inches in diameter. This is torn in two to form two bands. One of these two bands is next taken and torn in two, but instead of coming out two pieces, it comes out two pieces linked together. The next piece is then taken and torn in two, and instead of coming out two pieces, as it apparently should, it changes to one large piece, twice the size of the original. The effect is most bewildering and the trick is easy to perform. No skill of any kind is required. Comes complete with a presentation routine and enough equipment for two performances.

$3

Warner's Magic Factory
Box 455
Hinsdale, Ill. 60521

SCARFROPE

You are standing casually playing with a piece of rope. Suddenly, you can get the rope to become stiff and stand straight up in the air—like the Indian rope trick. At your command and by blowing on it, the rope will again become soft and fall down. And now a most interesting thing happens! Just by running your fingers softly over the edges of the rope, it changes immediately into a large silk scarf!

$3.50

Guaranteed Magic
27 Bright Rd.
Hatboro, Pa. 19040

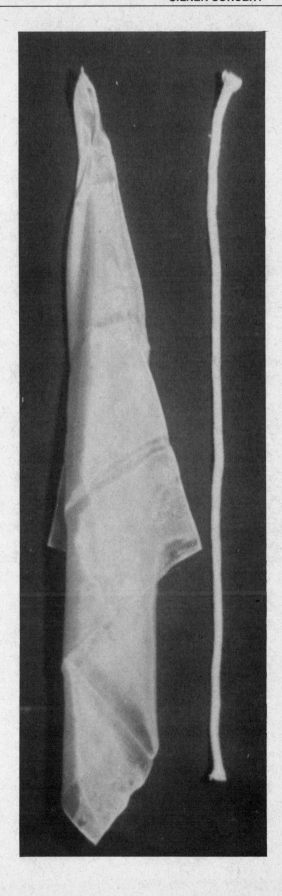

SUPER SWORD BOX

A classic in the world of magic. Remove the sword and the box instantly fills with silk. Place in the flap and the silk instantly vanishes. Measures 10×8×8 inches and has a heavy metal sword blade.

$12.50

Zanadu
165 Hancock Ave.
Jersey City, N.J. 07307

$17

Zanadu
165 Hancock Ave.
Jersey City, N.J. 07307

KRIPTAL KUBE

Put real magic in your life. Show a clear cube that is empty and fully closed. Hold it on the palm of your hand and at your command it is filled with silks or spring flowers. The 6-inch cube is precision-cut in Plexiglas with mitered edges to ensure strength and ease in assembly.

COLOR-CHANGING PLUMES

A truly beautiful creation of magic sure to be a positive hit in any program, as it is adaptable to both a silent or patter act.

A colored feather plume, say blue, is displayed to the audience. Next a sheet of paper is shown and fashioned into a tube. The plume is inserted into the tube and lo! When it emerges it has transformed into a brilliant orange plume!

The effect continues with yet another, different-colored plume being placed into the tube, and it, too, changing its color. In fact, the whole business is repeated with six plumes, each one changing to another color! The paper tube can be continually shown completely empty during the course of the routine, and in the end it is actually crushed and can be tossed out to the audience!

The fine-quality feather plumes with their brilliant colors make this a very beautiful and mystifying effect. Only six plumes are used—it's self-contained and very easy to do! You'll find you can even routine it into some of your other effects, such as silk dyeing, liquid effects, etc.

The color-changing plumes come to you complete with full instructions, routine, and everything needed to perform this right away.

$35

Micky Hades International
Box 2242
Seattle, Wash. 98111

SILK IN THE MIDDLE

This is the instantaneous and visible appearance of silk. A 12-inch red silk is put in one end of a clear tube, and a 12-inch blue silk is put in the other end. Suddenly, a white silk appears between the other two. Immediately all silks are blown out high into the air. Everything can be closely examined.

$11

Glenn Comar
353 E. Sixth Ave.
Roselle, N.J. 07203

ONE-HANDED CHANGING BAG

This is an all-purpose effect that can be used to make silks appear, disappear, or change into something else. You show an attractive little bag on the end of a handle. The bag is made of black velveteen and can be shown empty at any time you want. With a small movement of your finger you can make something in it appear, or something disappear. Do both at once and your silks have changed into a single large one, etc.

Comes complete with a pamphlet, "27 Tricks with a Changing Bag." This is an easy-to-work all-purpose prop.

$22

Glenn Comar
353 E. Sixth Ave.
Roselle, N.J. 07203

VISIBLE SILK IN BALLOON

A large, inflated, almost transparent balloon is shown to be quite empty. Now a silk is caused to vanish, and before you can blink your eye, it reappears inside the balloon. That's just the beginning. First of all, the silk is only half inside the balloon. The other half is outside. Not through the mouth of the balloon, but through the side! This is completely impossible, of course. At this point you grasp the silk by a corner and pull it slowly and completely out of the balloon, leaving the balloon intact and the silk in your hand.

Comes with twelve balloons and all the little things necessary to make it work. Can be used with the super needle balloon trick.

$7.50

Lou Tannen
1540 Broadway
New York, N.Y. 10036

$18.50

Flosso Hornmann
304 W. 34th St.
New York, N.Y. 10001

DEVIL'S SCARF-GO

A large, 24-inch beautifully colored scarf is shown outstretched between both hands. The four corners are brought up together in one hand. A dove is placed within the folds of the scarf, which is immediately shaken and opened up. Both sides are shown—the bird has vanished.

$15.90

Elmo Magic Supreme
1753 E. 16th St.
Brooklyn, N.Y. 11229

YOU'RE SEEING THINGS

A red silk is pushed into the hand and changes to green. But the audience sees a portion of the red silk showing, and when the silk is displayed it is half red and half green. When this is pushed

CRYSTAL SILK CYLINDER

Three orange silks are dropped into a clear 12×3-inch plastic cylinder. The cylinder is covered with a metal tube, and when it is removed the silks have changed into three real oranges. This is a real piece of stage magic as flashy and classy as it is baffling. Many other uses are possible. It can be used to switch silks or to change a red, white, and blue silk into an American flag, etc.

back into the hand it emerges red again. The magician says he will explain how the trick is done, but at the end he produces a piece of rope and says he has just been "stringing them along."

$5

Glenn Comar
353 E. Sixth Ave.
Roselle, N.J. 07203

BLENDO

A magic classic like this is hard to beat for sheer flash. Three different silks are shown and counted. Suddenly they are changed into one gorgeous silk that is 2 feet square. All three colors of the original silks are now included in the big one. The special silk does it all.

$17.50

Glenn Comar
353 E. Sixth Ave.
Roselle, N. J. 07203